The Disappearance of Danielle Imbo

Pete Dove

Published by Trellis Publishing, 2021.

THE DISAPPEARANCE OF DANIELLE IMBO

First edition. July 3, 2021.

ISBN: 979-8224821013

Written by Pete Dove.

THE DISAPPEARANCE OF DANIELLE IMBO

Pete Dove

Lost without trace

A ticket to the Superbowl can be a big thing. Especially if you are a fan. A reason for divorce, though? It is hard to see that. Unless, as in the case of Joe Imbo and his then wife, Danielle, it is the straw that breaks a marriage's back.

It did not help, of course, that Danielle was ill at the time, and had been left behind to look after their infant son who was also suffering from a cold. Not an especially unusual or worrying occurrence, of course, but anybody who has cared for a small child suffering from an illness such as this will know how cranky and miserable it can make them. The baby does not understand that it is suffering from a minor ailment and will recover soon. It cannot be drenched in cold cure powders, or paracetamol. So, feeling uncomfortable, unable to breathe easily and with a headache and perhaps a sore throat, the baby whines. Continuously. Endlessly. It will not rest, cannot even relax when held but instead struggles and wriggles in its parents' arms.

As hard as we try, it is tricky to make out that a baby with a cold is a big problem. But we all know that if we are left to care for that baby without support, and are feeling ill ourselves, the problem such as it is magnifies in our head. We long for respite; for a moment to ourselves.

It seems as though, to Joe, the ticket to the Superbowl was more important than offering help to his wife. And son. That is not a crime. Maybe, though, it is an act of selfishness. It is also, very probably, the act of a man who feels that his marriage is breaking down, and that he wants out. Joe later told Danielle that he happened to meet a woman on the flight to the Superbowl, and the two hit it off. It was the end of the road. Goodbye.

The couple, though, did not have time to divorce. Danielle had disappeared before that could happen. Even if such permanent separation was on the cards. Joe learned, to his cost, that romance which blossoms up in the skies can lack solid foundations. The mile-high club is not all it is cut out to be. What had seemed so promising squashed together in Economy class proved less attractive when played out in more space. Joe and the woman stayed together for only a short time. Then Joe got back in touch with Danielle. How about giving marriage a second chance? The proposal was made, but matters were more complicated than that for his wife.

Two decades before Danielle Ottobre, as she was then, had started High School as a fresh-faced young teen. She had soon teamed up with another girl, Christine Petrone. The friendship would endure well beyond the end of schooldays. Christine's father ran a small bakery in town. She also had an older brother; he was friendly enough, but the young Danielle had no interest in him.

Years on, Danielle was married, and in her own uncertain relationship. Richard, too, had been involved with a woman and had a fourteen-year-old daughter from that. By this stage he was running the family business. Currently, that duty falls to the now adult daughter. Vikings Pastries, which is based in Ardmore, Pennsylvania, has a good reputation locally. Meanwhile, the situation with Joe was looking bad. Although he was the one who had stepped away from the relationship, he was fighting for custody of their son. With the threat of divorce, a custody battle and all the issues around being a single mom, Danielle was looking for support. She worked as a mortgage consultant, a steady enough job but not one which bristled with financial benefits.

It was during this tricky time, and before Joe decided he would like them to get back together again, that she and Richard realised that there might be more between then than is usual with an older brother of a best friend. The two began dating. It seemed like an easy enough relationship. So much so, that when Joe made the contact and suggested that they come back together, Richard recognised the dilemma in his girlfriend's mind, and was happy to step away so that each could resume their old roles.

Perhaps that is a mark of a very fine, very considerate man. Perhaps it is also a sign that the relationship was fun, but not destined to last forever. We do not know. In fact, not knowing is a theme that will resurface again and again in this story of missing persons, presumed dead.

It was a Saturday evening in February 2005. The nineteenth, to be precise. Richard was at home, alone, and planning on what he could do that night. There was live music on in town, and he texted his sister to see if she would like to go and listen to it with him. She, though, had stuff on that night and could not make it. Christine was not alone at the time, Danielle was with her, and she passed on her brother's message. Although Danielle and Richard had not seen each other for a month – had not spoken, in fact – it seemed as though they had an easy relationship. What about Danielle going to the music event in her place?

Danielle liked the idea, and Richard arranged to pick her up. It seemed as though they had a good night. The music was happening at Abilene's, a bar in South Street. That garishly fronted building, decorated in swatches of red and yellow, with a seventies style information pane atop the wall, no longer exists. The building was demolished some time ago. Architecturally, it is unlikely to be missed. Nevertheless, the couple sat close together, shared an occasional kiss. To witnesses spoken to later, they looked like a typical youngish couple, in love, close and comfortable with each other. They had, in fact, met up with friends and shared a table at the Philadelphia bar. Danielle lived, at the time, in a condo in Mount Laurel. That was about twenty-five minutes away from South Street, and the arrangements as Christine knew them were that Richard would drive his date – it seems as though that was what their night out had become – home there afterwards. Witnesses report them leaving the bar at around 11.45 pm. Richard's four-year-old black Dodge Dakota pick-up was parked nearby.

And there the story goes cold. Nobody has seen Danielle Imbo since that time. Nor Richard Petrone. Nor the pick-up truck. That, according to the FBI, is perhaps the most unusual element of the case. People go missing. It is sad, but true. Their vehicle is usually found. And quickly.

Richard had plans for the next day. He was a bit of a motor racing fan, and on Sunday was the NASCAR Daytona 500. He planned to settle down with a couple of beers and enjoy the spectacle from the comfort of his armchair in front of the TV. A definite scheme, although one that would be straightforward to change, if circumstances dictated. For Danielle, plans were a little more concrete. She had a hair appointment arranged for the morning, but never appeared for her 11.00 am slot. More significantly, perhaps, Joe was dropping off their son in the afternoon. Everybody who knew her confirmed that there was nothing that would stop her from being home for that. Remember, she was entering a custody battle for her son, which provided an even stronger reason for her to be there when he arrived. Little Joe was by far the most important person in her life.

On the Sunday, John Ottobre, Danielle's brother, popped round. He was surprised to find the house locked up and dark. He phoned his sister, to check that she was OK and to find out where she was. The call went unanswered and switched quickly to voice mail. When his own family attempted to contact Richard, the same outcome occurred. Indeed, neither cell phone was used again, and nor were the credit cards of either person.

Did the couple make it back to the car? Did they reach Danielle's home? Were they intercepted on the way there? Did they choose to disappear? The answers to these, and just about every other question on the lips of investigators receives the same response. Unknown. Insufficient information. There is no evidence to suggest that the couple did get back to Danielle's condo, and certainly that they went inside. There is nothing to suggest that they left the bar on anything other than good terms. Not even excessively good ones, which might have raised an eyebrow. There is no hint of obsession on either of their parts. Two good friends, experiencing what their mates called an 'on again, off again' relationship, enjoying one of the 'on again' phases.

The case was initially investigated by the local police, before being passed on to the FBI. It now features high up in their list of missing persons investigations. It seems as though six main theories have emerged regarding what could have happened to Danielle and Richard.

These are, in no particular order, the start a new life theory; the angry ex-theory, which evolves into speculative lines of the greedy ex, jealous ex and 'there is no suspicion at all of the ex being involved which makes him the most likely perpetrator' theory. The third hypothesis is partly linked to the unlikely one above and sits under the vague heading of the 'murder for hire' theory. Fourth is the random crime supposition, with its close cousin, which follows on that somebody was after the Dodge Dakota, and poor Richard and Danielle just got in the way. Fifth on the list are the arguments put forward by those wanting to blame 'the mob' for the killings. Finally, the cold-water theory, which suggests the car was involved in an accident and plunged into one of the main icy waterways and lakes which lie between Philadelphia and Danielle's home in Mount Laurel, New Jersey. Unfortunately, it is not just this last supposition on which it is far too easy to pour the kind of chilly water which exists in rivers in icy Philadelphia in February. All of the scenarios have considerably more reasons against them than ones which suggest they might provide the answer.

Of course, sadly, all but the first of these hypotheses lead to the inevitable conclusion that Danielle and Richard are dead. That this is the conclusion reached by all but the most 'conspiracy theory' orientated of interested parties says as much about the credibility given to the idea that the couple set up home together as it does about the tragedy of their respective demise.

Still, it is worth spending a little time considering the possibility that the couple decided to run away together, if only to show how ludicrous such a theory is. It requires both to give up children that they love; it requires Richard to abandon the family business. It requires his Dodge Dakota to disappear off of the face of the earth. It requires them to have set up alternative lives, with new credit cards and phones. Most ludicrously of all, it requires their date that night not to have emerged by chance. Instead, Richard and Danielle would need to have planned that Richard contact his sister with a suggestion that they meet up and go to a bar to watch some live music, but to make that offer in the knowledge that she would turn it down. Also, for Danielle to happen to be around when the suggestion is made. Finally, for Christine to make the uncertain step to invite her best friend to accompany her brother on the outing.

No, there is no possibility that Richard and Danielle decided to abscond, and therefore, no possibility that they are still alive. Two children grew up without their respective parents. They will not see them, alive, again.

But could Joe Imbo, drawn into a custody battle for his son, rejected in his appeal to get back together again with Danielle, have decided to carry out the ultimate revenge? Of course, the possibility cannot be dismissed. Most murders are committed by people known to the victim. Trawl through speculative websites and read the comments of their often-illusory readers and it seems that such suspicion is well founded.

'Ex-husband for sure!' states Eric on the True Crime Guy website. He is so confident he even adds an exclamation mark. The interestingly monikered B. Speeg takes the speculation further. 'Here's the general scenario with these situations in our society:' he notes with exemplary punctuation and total assertion, 'Dad's (sic – the punctuation starts to slip at this point) who are going through divorce are WITH the kids when they visit - - not out partying.' Mr or Mrs/Ms Speeg seem to have gotten a little excited, judging by the double hyphen and capitals, although unfortunately that is the extent of their argument. It seems as though they, and others on this and similar sites, find it suspicious that the father went out to a party, leaving his infant son to sleep under the care of babysitters. They imply this is evidence of his guilt and it has been wilful negligence on the part of the police not to have arrested him on the spot. Presumably, though, the evidence of other party goers negated such action.

Indeed, the party Joe Imbo attended that night was almost equidistant from both Philadelphia's South Street and his wife's home – about fifty miles from each. It seems as though he then went to stay with his mom for the night, who was carrying out the babysitting duties. Grandma babysitting for a child! There's something suspicious! A scenario rarely encountered. However, these flights of fantasy pay no heed to another fact; the party Joe attended was not some drunken rave, but a children's birthday party. And he did not go there alone, so that he might slip away. He went with his stepfather. A retired member of the New York Police Department.

Yet those who seek to blame the partner whenever a spouse goes missing see such apparent proof of innocence as evidence of guilt. Joe Imbo planned his alibi too carefully. Joe Imbo relied on his mom for cover. Signs of guilt, both. Such conclusions conveniently overlook the fact that Joe could not have carried out the crimes himself, because the time scales do not fit. That even if he had, he would then face the problem of disposing of a large black Dodge Dakota whilst also having his own vehicle with him and would require a number of people, including his own mother, to lie on his behalf.

'He hired a killer,' they shout in a moment of righteous discovery. If so, he found a remarkably talented assassin. Who offered good value as well. One capable not only of killing two people and disposing of their bodies, but also a pick-up. As another respondent on social media states, such a hit would require 'a lot of coin.'

Expounding on such theories must be hard for Joe and his family, even though it is an inevitable consequence of crime. But when it comes to evidence, there is just none that Joe was the killer. He had no means to carry out such a crime, and only the most minimal of motives. He also had a strong alibi which placed him a long way from the action. In fact, the only possible indicator of any antipathy from Joe are reports of some telephone arguments with Richard Pestone. Still, Imbo does not come out of the marriage break up well, but that is many miles away from grounds for suspecting he is responsible for the deaths of his wife and her boyfriend.

Nevertheless, it is the murder for hire theory that the FBI considers the strongest of all the possibilities. Their conclusion is reached not because they suspect Joe of being behind the crime. More that it is the disappearance of the Dakota which is hardest to explain. Bodies are relatively small, and relatively easy to chop up and bury or hide. A large pick-up is not. Yes, there are workshops which specialise in dismantling vehicles and selling them off as spares. But these tend to be older vehicles, or ones caught up in accidents. Not four-year-old cars in a good state of repair. To chop up such a vehicle would undoubtedly promote questions and stick in the mind. Investigators spoke with every such demolition yard in the area, and none reported the Dakota as having passed through their company. Surely, as the news of the double disappearance spread, anybody who handled the vehicle would have reported it.

The pick-up's VIN number is engraved on every panel, every significant moving part, just about. It is hard to believe that the car could have been broken up, distributed, refitted into other vehicles and never have come to light. When Dr Frankenstein created his monster, it was spotted everywhere it went – even as far as the Arctic Circle. But Richard's Dodge Dakota simply, like its owner, disappeared and has never resurfaced.

Carjacking is not an unheard of crime. Mostly, this occurs when vehicles are stolen to order. A new Range Rover, or Mercedes might attract the attention of thieves with a buyer ready and waiting to take possession. Such an outcome remains a possibility for the car in which

Richard and Danielle travelled to the South Street bar back in the icy night of February 19th, 2005. Again, though, it seems unlikely. As nice as though a four-year-old pick-up truck might be to own, it is hardly the kind of vehicle which promotes a mass demand on the black market. It is possible that, if somebody did indeed take the vehicle, they needed it for a specific purpose. A crime, perhaps, where a strong, sturdy means of transport was needed, but one which would not stand out in a crowd. So perhaps a carjacking gone wrong is one of the more serious contenders among the possibilities the authorities considered.

Did Richard protest as somebody attempted to steal the vehicle? Did he discover an attempted theft from the parking spot he had found before heading to the bar? That option too was investigated and dismissed. While it was late at night that he and Danielle returned to the vehicle, Richard had been pleased that he had found a parking spot close to the venue, which was in a busy part of town. It is impossible to believe that the vehicle was stolen, and two people murdered, in such close proximity to a busy street.

Thus, the car-jacking possibility remains the more likely option. Philadelphia is not especially renowned as a violent or crime ridden city, but like anywhere else with a large population, there are sectors which are best avoided late at night. One of these is the borough of Camden, which has one of the highest crime rates in the state. In fact, there are few areas in the whole of the United States which are considered more dangerous when it comes to violent crime. There are many routes Richard could have chosen to take Danielle home, and one of them passes straight through the centre of this unsafe area.

It is unlikely that Richard inadvertently chose to drive through this run-down suburb, but anybody can take a wrong turning, end up on a route across a bridge they would rather avoid. Could that have been the Ben Franklin bridge, and from there, did Richard – maybe tired, or a little confused from alcohol – ended up where he did not want them to be?

There are many ways, unfortunately, through which it can be imagined that a scenario escalated. An insurance fraud bump; a robbery at a traffic light. Getting lost in the tight streets around the area. There are plenty of ways this might happen. Although, once more, what happens to the vehicle remains a challenging question.

Which leads onto the fifth consideration of which the authorities took account. Might there be the possibility that Richard and Danielle – the latter simply through the chance of being there in the wrong place at the wrong time -became the victims of a planned and organised hit? But not one paid for by the ex-husband of the innocent woman, but rather because Richard had run foul of an organised criminal group? The mob, it is widely held, are a powerful influence on the underworld of many parts of Philadelphia. Could they be responsible for both deaths? And the disappearance of the car?

The mob is certainly an organisation – one of the very few – which might be able to perpetrate these acts – and get away with it. Vito Roselli was the FBI officer in charge of the case and said, as reported in Philadelphia Magazine back in 2014: 'Making two people and a truck disappear, with no witnesses and no evidence of any kind of nine years suggests methodical planning.' In fact, the FBI had first made public their belief that the couple were killed in a 'murder for hire' plot as far back as 2008, just three years after they disappeared. The grounds seem to centre around two unrelated facts, neither of them especially strong. The first is simply that the mob were known to operate in and around the parts of Philadelphia where Richard frequented. Secondly, the fact that he ran the sort of small business that might attract the attentions of racketeers.

Running a bakery might appear as quite a pleasant job; creative, one which provides customer satisfaction and so forth. However, a lot of buns must be sold to make a profit. Had Viking Pastries run into debt? Did it owe money to the mobsters? Was Richard killed as a warning to others?

This seems a somewhat melodramatic path to follow. Certainly, nothing reported about Richard's behaviour that night in the Abilene bar suggested a man in fear of his life. And would a person in such a frightening hole really invite his sister out for a late night in the centre of Philadelphia? And then transfer that invitation to the mother of a small child when his sister cannot attend?

For a short time, it was even mooted that a different kind of organised crime gang might have been behind the killings. Facing trial for the supply of illegal pills, a member of the Pagan motorcycle gang was questioned about a double homicide. Reporters and other armchair sleuths added up the fact and arrived at an unlikely answer. The double homicide – crimes which were totally denied by the alleged perpetrator in any case – was of Danielle and Richard. Putting two and two together and making sixty-three as the answer. Fortunately, that particular theory was quickly abandoned.

It seems as though a lot of desperate straw clutching has taken place. Which leads to the final option investigators have considered over the intervening years. That Richard crashed his car and ended up in one of the many freezing waterways that flow through the border area between Pennsylvania and New Jersey. Dangerous at any time of year, these fast-flowing rivers and deep pools become treacherous when the temperature falls, and water levels rise.

No reports of an accident came in that night that might be linked to Richard's Dakota; but then since neither couple nor car were spotted on any CCTV cameras, this does not completely rule out the possibility of an accident.

More, rivers were dredged, and lakes searched along the possible routes Richard might have followed to take his girlfriend home. Nothing turned up. But there was history of this kind of failure. In the sixties a group of teenagers disappeared on their way to a school dance. Nothing was found of them for forty years, until a dry spell lowered the water table to an extent that the rivers ran dry. Then a 67 Camaro emerged, with the white bones of the youngsters inside.

There are plenty of roads that Richard might have taken; there are plenty of places where a car could leave the road and crash over a bank and into the freezing depths. Fast flowing currents could take even a vehicle as large and heavy as the Dakota and place it elsewhere, out of the search of divers.

Maybe even now a black pick-up waits, its final occupants still inside. Perhaps one day water levels will fall again, and a Dodge Dakota will be discovered. We can only hope so. Although all accept that their loved ones are dead, there are two families, including a son and a daughter, who still await news. These are not siblings but are united by tragedy rather than the bond of step brothers and sisters.

There is still too much idle speculation about the disappearance of Danielle Imbo and Richard Pestone. Still too many silly ideas and stupid theories. They need to stop, and the truth that the couple died as a result of a terrible, but unremarkable in its way, accident will at least serve to end the gossip and put minds at rest. If not, peace.

AMBER Alert: The Murder of Amber Creek

RENEE DUCKWORTH

Amber Gail Creek, who preferred to be called 'Aimee', was born on July 2, 1982 in Park Ridge, Cook County, Illinois. Her parents had lived together for just two years and had never married by the time that they each went their separate ways. Amber lived with her mother, Elizabeth Mowers, in the village of Lake Zurich, a north-western residential suburb of Chicago, until she was six years old. This was far from a happy home. Her mother was a cocaine addict who would often use in front of her daughter. Amber also divulged that a man had sexually abused her whilst she was under her mother's care. The Illinois Department of Children and Family Services stepped in and Amber's father Robert Creek was awarded sole custody of his daughter. She was sent to live with him in the nearby suburb of Palatine.

It was here that Amber grew up. Contact between Amber and her mother was all but cut off. Initially she was haunted by memories of the abuse and would often cry herself to sleep at night. However, over time, and despite the abuse, separation of her parents and the shuffled living arrangements, Amber seemed (at least for the time being, and to outward appearances) to develop into a relatively cheerful child who led the regular life of a suburban girl. Her best friend and fellow Sundling Junior High School class of 1996 graduate, Heather Lowing, recalls Amber fondly - 'I remember her being happy. She was just a very normal, junior high girl. I don't remember her missing school because she ran away, or talking about an awful home life.'

However, within six months all of that would change. As she entered her freshman year of high school, Amber sunk into a deep and crippling depression. Seeking some kind of temporary relief from her despair, she turned to drugs and alcohol. 'She didn't want to deal with it,' Robert Creek later said. She would act out by repeatedly running away from home for brief stints or by sneaking out of the house at night to meet older boys. Her cousin, Desiree Reeves, recalls 'She told me she was in the woods with a few boys. I remember asking her, "Why? Why do you sneak out?" I was scared for her. I was.'

Amber's family photo album tells a sad story. Within that six month period, Amber changes from a smiling, long-haired, makeup-less, All-American girl next door wearing bright clothing, to a blank-staring, dark-dyed and short-haired, made-up Lolita wearing black. It is common for those suffering from depression to seek to change their image in the belief that by transforming themselves on the outside they can fix what is troubling them on the inside. Robert would later say Amber had 'spiralled down' during this period and that 'She did not have the ability to keep relationships.'

By December of 1996, Amber's self-destructive behavior had worsened to the point where her psychiatrist recommended an intensive course of residential therapy. Robert Creek was unable to afford the hefty $50,000 price tag to follow up on the recommended form of therapy, instead attaining outpatient therapy for his daughter through a local hospital. His insurance did not cover this therapy for very long though, and when it ran out, he says 'She would come back home and the problems started again. Our psychiatrist wanted her in a locked-in facility. He said - and these are his exact words - "Someone is going to kill her if we do not do something." She was putting herself into more dangerous situations.'

Frustrated with the amount of red tape in the system, Robert pleaded with the DCFS to take Amber into their care but they refused. In a desperate move, he took her to the Palatine Police Department and told the officers present that Amber could no longer live in his house. This forced the DCFS' hand. Robert relinquished Amber into their temporary custody as a ward of the state. Subsequent unsuccessful attempts to place Amber in a foster home saw her entered into a group home situation at a North Chicago youth shelter, the Columbus-Maryville Center.

Amber continued her chronic runaway behavior during her stay at the center. By late 1996 she had ran away nine times, staying for only twenty-nine of the forty-four days that she was supposed to be living there. When she would run away, she would inevitably return to her father's home. On January 23, 1997, Amber ran away again. This time, she would never return home. Robert sensed that his troubled daughter had ran away for good this time - 'I knew when she was gone. She would have called home. She was never gone more than three days.' Amber did place phone calls to other relatives during this time, but she refused to reveal where she was staying. Attempting to make it on her own on the mean streets of Chicago, and without any money with which to purchase food to fill her belly, sadly Amber resorted to prostitution in desperation. On Saturday February 1, 1997, Amber's new wild lifestyle found her attending a weekend-long booze-soaked party at a Motel 6 with a group of older men in Rolling Meadows. At one point some police officers attended the party to perform a regulation check-up but they did not spot Amber, nor were they aware that she was currently a missing person whom they should have picked up if they had have seen her. Amber was witnessed leaving the party with a Caucasian male aged in his 30s. He was clean-shaven, of average height and medium to heavy build with brown hair and eyes. He was wearing a shirt and tie. They drove away in a large, gray, late model four-door luxury car, possibly a Lincoln. It had gray leather seats and a placard on the dashboard reading 'Mayor' against a white background. This was the last time that Amber was seen alive.

On February 9, 1997, a pair of men hunting in the Karcher Wildlife Area in the town of Burlington, Wisconsin made a gruesome discovery. Amber's frozen and battered corpse was lying in a marsh. It had been a brutal death and the killer seemed to have posed the body. It appeared to be a sexually motivated homicide. She had been bashed and raped, bitten savagely on the neck with great force and slashed about the face. She had been suffocated with a garbage bag which she still wore around her head. One arm was propped up against a tree as if to mimic a friendly wave and the word 'Hi' was written on her palm in black marker. Also affixed to her arm was a $5 price tag that had come from a *Golden Book* sold at a bookstore in Woodfield Mall in Schaumberg, Illinois.

The killer may have been signifying that Amber was cheap garbage. Some interpret the message as 'High-5.' Racine County Sheriff Chris Schmaling would later comment 'I'll tell you one thing: she did not deserve this. To be left here, just left like trash. It's sad and tragic. I have a 14-year-old daughter at home. I can't imagine if I lost her. Amber's parents looked all over Illinois. Her dad searched the streets. I don't think it would have crossed his mind that his daughter was lying dead in the cold in Wisconsin. I can't even fathom what that must be like. That's one reason why this case has never gone cold. It's so easy to forget about these cases after a couple decades, but I refuse to shelve these cases.'

Amber's body may have been posed as a sick joke intended to shock whoever eventually found her. She was naked from the waist down. The pants Amber had been wearing were discovered in a nearby parking lot with her panties stuffed into one of the pockets. Conspicuously absent were two possessions that Amber was never seen without - her distinctive forest-green winter jacket with a leather lapel and her dark green backpack on which she had drawn the 'Starter' logo in pencil. Within was poetry she wrote, cosmetics and photographs of her half-siblings. The murderer may have taken these items as trophies and to fuel later sexual homicide fantasies. Investigators gathered that Amber had been killed by one of her johns. At a 1999 FBI National Center for the Analysis of Violent Crime regional training conference, a member of the Amber Creek Homicide Task Force stated that 'because of Amber's high-risk lifestyle as a chronic runaway and prostitute who engaged in drug use, it was very possible that one of her clients had killed her.' Friends of Amber dispute the claims that she was a prostitute and drug addict. After the grisly find, investigators hid cameras in the area in an effort to capture the killer in case they returned to the scene of the crime, but no one did.

Amber was not identified immediately. The Columbus-Maryville Center failed to report her missing for a full five weeks after she disappeared from the shelter. When they did finally file the report they provided the wrong girl's photograph. Amber became a Jane Doe, and it was under this placeholder name that she was buried. The sad story of the unidentified, pretty, young murder victim that no one had claimed hit the headlines and touched the community. One hundred Wisconsinites turned out to Jane Doe's funeral so that the unfortunate girl might have someone to mourn her passing. A local man who had been moved by the story donated the casket and sheriff's deputies served as pallbearers.

Unaware that his daughter was dead by this stage, Robert Creek drove around Chicago and its suburbs searching for Amber for more than a year – 'It's a terrible thing to be driving around and see someone and have to turn back to see if it was her... It never was.'

Investigators had expended thousands of man-hours attempting to match fingerprints, DNA and dental records to their missing person files to no avail. It would take until June 26, 1998 for Amber's body to be positively identified through dental and DNA matches. *America's Most Wanted* had profiled the case that year. Robert Creek had viewed the episode and contacted police to inform them that he believed that Jane Doe was his daughter. When authorities finally realized who they had, more than a year after her death, Amber was reburied with a new, personal headstone at Holy Family Catholic Cemetery, Caledonia, Wisconsin. The stone reads: *Amber Creek, July 1982 – Feb. 1997. Earth has no sorrow that Heaven cannot heal, "You are so loved."*

Realizing that the Columbus-Maryville Center's initial inaction and mistakes had hindered the investigation, state laws regarding reporting of runaways were altered in direct response to Amber's case to prevent this from happening again. Illinois social workers initially denied that they had delayed reporting the disappearance. The Illinois DCFS insisted the disappearance was reported promptly on January

23, 1997. A Chicago police spokesperson said that there was no report filed that day.

Early investigations after Amber's identification focused on a pair of local men who often ran afoul of the Palatine and Rolling Meadows police departments, and who had also been in attendance at the Motel 6 party. However, DNA analysis eventually cleared these men of any wrongdoing. Fliers were distributed, a hotline was opened and fingerprint samples from the garbage bag were sent to the FBI and law enforcement agencies in 49 states. Detective John Hanrahan said 'Whoever killed Amber has kind of relaxed and settled in and no one came knocking. I can only imagine his stress level must be rising knowing that sooner or later we'll be knocking on his door.' For some time investigators ran out of leads to pursue and Amber's murder investigation stagnated.

In October of 2013 an Oklahoma forensics laboratory started to re-examine fingerprints lifted from various unsolved homicide cases. In February of 2014 the case was re-opened when Stacy Hirschman, an examiner at the Oklahoma laboratory, got a hit on a thumbprint found on the garbage bag that had covered Amber's face. It belonged to one James Paul Eaton, a 36-year-old Chicago Private Bank & Trust Company employee from Palatine. He had an ex-wife of 3 ½ years. The couple did not have any children. Eaton was nineteen years old at the time of Amber's death and his description closely resembled that of a man seen with Amber in February 1997. Eaton's fingerprints had not been matched at the time Amber's body was discovered as he was not in the system yet. He had not had any dealings with police until a 2000 arrest for possession of drug paraphernalia.

Hirschman contacted Agent Eric Szatkowski of the Wisconsin Department of Justice's Criminal Investigation Division to report the matched print. He was shocked when he heard the news - 'I literally almost fell off my chair in my office!' Investigators tracked Eaton down in Chicago and began several days of surveillance on him. On a March

22 stakeout they witnessed Eaton smoke several cigarettes outside the downtown Palatine Metra train station whilst he awaited his train which was running late, discarding the butts on the ground as he finished them. When Eaton left the scene the investigators recovered the cigarette butts. DNA from the cigarette butts was then matched to semen recovered through rectal swabbing at the crime scene. Police arrested Eaton in early April. Stacy Hirschman said 'I saw the print and just did my job and searched it, just wanting to ID that print. I'm just glad he's off the streets. Hopefully the family can have some peace.' Amber's aunt as well as family friends called Hirschman to personally thank her. A colleague had bet her a dinner that she would not get a hit on the almost two-decade-old fingerprints – 'He was quite stunned. He was silent for a bit. He definitely owed me dinner.' During interrogation, investigators endeavored to elicit an admission of guilt from Eaton. They showed him pictures of Amber while she was still alive. Eaton calmly denied ever having met her. They showed him crime scene pictures of Amber's body. He did not display a reaction.

Racine County Sheriff Christopher Schmaling told the media 'Today by far was the best moment for my investigative team as we informed Amber's dad that we caught her killer. It was an emotional exchange for everyone in the room. I couldn't be more proud of my investigative team today. Their hard work and commitment is unmatched. Today is a fantastic day to make a wonderful announcement to bring some closure to the Creek family. This is a day that we have been waiting more than seventeen years to arrive. We have solid, clear and overwhelming evidence that the suspect was responsible for Creek's death. Over the last seventeen years we have dedicated thousands of investigative hours to bring this tragic and senseless murder to its resolution. Today that day is here. Eaton had not previously been a suspect, nor was he even mentioned in our investigative reports. Our sense of accomplishment is tempered by the pain and loss we know Amber's family continues to confront every day.

Our thoughts and prayers remain with Amber's father, mother, other family and loved ones. We believe there are people out there who have knowledge of Mr Eaton and his involvement in the crime. We ask those people to search their hearts, do the right thing for Amber and her family, and come forward. While it is a great moment for the family to have closure, they are also asking for privacy to deal with their grief.' Palatine police Commander Dave Daigle echoed these sentiments – 'We have never arrested him. The only contact we've had is he received a speeding ticket and he was a victim of a burglary to his motor vehicle.'

Amber's aunt, Nowra Mowers said 'We are elated, absolutely, that someone has been caught in this crime. We've been waiting seventeen years. After seventeen years, my sister never gave up hope and my mother did not. She did not deserve to die in this way. Nobody deserves to die in this way. I want to know about him. Did he kill other people? Is she the only victim?'

Racine County Chief Deputy John Hanrahan, who was one of the top investigators in Amber's case from the beginning, gave a scathing indictment of the DCFS' handling of Amber's case at the time of her disappearance – 'Not only was the care and security they provided her extraordinarily inadequate, their failure to report Amber missing until well after she was found murdered is simply incredible. Amber and her family deserved much more.' Hanrahan had previously told the media in 1999 'Delays in identifying Amber's body have put us behind the 8-ball when it comes to tracking her killer. I believe this is a solvable case. I've got twenty years before I leave. This case will be worked on for at least the next twenty years.'

Many people, including Amber's uncle Anthony Mowers, believe that Eaton did not act alone in the murder. He speculates that Eaton may have had assistance in crossing interstate with Amber and that they may have lured Amber into a car under the pretence of offering her a lift to her grandmother's house (the grandmother lived in Wisconsin at the time). Police share Mowers' suspicion that Eaton did not act alone.

It is currently unknown if the human bite mark on Amber's neck came from Eaton, fuelling public speculation that Eaton had an accomplice or accomplices. Eaton's saliva, however, was located at the crime scene.

One of those present at a pre-trial hearing was Anthony Mowers, who stated 'I'm here for Amber. Just imagine how scared she must have been. I have no clue who this guy is. Nobody in the family does. This guy had to know this area. I don't know how the hell he got to that spot. He had to have somebody else along. Why would he drive there? How did he find this place? That's what I'm wondering, if it was some sort of partying. I wonder if he's got an ace up his sleeve. He's gotta have another perp involved. I don't understand - this guy's from Palatine. Maybe she thought he was taking her to her grandmother's house. There's no way she would have been in the car with him that long. At least not without putting up a fight. I'm still thinking he killed her in Illinois.'

Eaton shuffled into the hearing clad in orange Racine County Jail scrubs and sat quietly with his head down throughout the proceedings, while Mowers struggled to barely contain his rage, glaring at Eaton and clenching his jaw all the while. Racine County District Attorney Rich Chiapete pointed to Eaton and said 'This is an individual that has hid from the law for seventeen years. This case is chilling. It is a sad, savage, brutal attack. The bite mark was so significant it was a major and primary cause of her death here. We have an innocent, 14-year-old victim here. She was dumped like she was garbage.'

Amber's mother told the press 'Oh God, I knew I should have taken her. I didn't think they'd ever find this person. I'm so happy for that.' Her decision not to re-apply for custody of Amber at the time when she was placed in state care haunts her to this day. Eaton was held in the Racine County jail on $1 million bail. After the hearing Anthony Mowers exploded at a Racine County sheriff's investigator who walked up to him outside the courtroom and asked for his name. Mowers began yelling and ranting at the plain clothed investigator before storming out. But Mowers later hugged the man after realizing that he had investigating Amber's death and wanted to discuss the case. Mowers had mistaken the man for an Eaton supporter – 'He stared me down in the courtroom. I thought it was one of the Eaton family members. He shouldn't have come at me like that. I'm looking at a monster that killed my niece.'

Eaton was charged with murder one and concealing a body, which would have attracted a life sentence in prison. In October of 2014 Eaton pleaded not guilty to both charges at his arraignment. The trial proper was to begin in November 2015. Defense for the accused argued that the prosecution had not made available all of its evidence at discovery. The trial was then delayed until June 6, 2016 as the defense tried to find a man they contended had bitten Amber's neck so as to inspect his potential dental match as well as compare his DNA to that recovered at the crime scene. The judge threw out certain evidence supplied by the prosecution in relation to Eaton's interrogation when Eaton's attorney successfully argued that police had denied Eaton's requests to speak to a lawyer. In ignoring this request and continuing to interrogate Eaton, anything he might have said after that point was not permissible in court – 'Mr Eaton unequivocally and unambiguously invoked his right to counsel on April 5. At that point, all interrogation and questioning of Mr Eaton was to cease,' Racine County Circuit Court Judge Eugene Gasiorkiewicz said. The requests for counsel in question made by Eaton are as follows: 1 – 'I really think you guys need to get me a lawyer 'cause this is getting crazy;' 2 – 'I think you guys need to get me a lawyer 'cause this is crazy;' and 3 – 'I need to talk to a lawyer.'

It was only after Eaton's third request that detectives suspended the interrogation. Sheriff's Investigator Thomas Knaus testified that he ceased interrogating Eaton on April 5 after the third time he requested to speak to a lawyer. Knaus said that he had originally given Eaton a telephone book so that he could call a lawyer himself - 'I think he said he didn't have an attorney, so he didn't accept the phone book.' Upon cross-examination Knaus also admitted that he did not allow Eaton the opportunity to contact family members for the purposes of hiring a lawyer, nor did he call the Cook County Public Defender's Office to organize for a lawyer to meet with Eaton. Judge Gasiorkiewicz said that by investigators continuing to interrogate Eaton after his requests they had violated of his Fifth and Sixth Amendment rights, which pertain to not incriminating oneself and the right to a lawyer. Obviously it is not known what Eaton said during the time when the interrogation was in violation, but during the hearing Judge Gasiorkiewicz did say that 'He denied any ability to recognize Amber. Mr Eaton did not physically react when shown those photos. They were unsuccessful in obtaining a confession.'

Eaton pleaded no contest to a lesser charge of first-degree reckless homicide on October 25, 2016. A plea of no contest occurs when a defendant neither admits nor denies the charges. It is rather an acknowledgement that the defendant concedes that the prosecution would likely be successful in gaining a conviction against them based on the evidence, were the case to go to trial. Whilst not technically a guilty plea, it has the same instant effect. At the time of writing Eaton has yet to be sentenced, but he is facing up to 40 years in prison once this takes place. He is currently imprisoned in Racine, Wisconsin. Whilst most people consider that Eaton murdered Amber Creek, he is not without his supporters. Some people posit that Eaton met Amber at the Motel 6 party, had consensual sex with her that night, gave her the plastic bag for whatever reason, and was killed by her pimp for failing to charge Eaton. A second man, whose name has not yet been released, is also currently under investigation for alleged connection to the crime.

WHEN THE GIRL NEXT DOOR KILLS: THE TRUE STORY OF TYLAR WITT

ERICA FOSTER

"At round one in the morning, the girl snuck the boy into her house. He stabbed her in her sleep, killing her and freeing themselves." This was an excerpt from fourteen year old Tylar Witt's story entitled, "The Killer and his Raven." A story she wrote about her own mother's brutal murder.

Tylar Witt lived in an upscale neighborhood in El Dorado Hills, California with her forty seven year old single mother, Joanne Witt. Joanne worked for the county as an assistant engineer for the Department of Transportation and they lived in an elegant house in a nice gated community. Tylar was a fourteen year old girl who was entering her freshman year at Oak Ridge High School. She was described as a sweet girl when she was growing up. Her mother paid for riding lessons and they liked to stay at home and watch movies and cook, but as Tylar grew up, the behavioral problems began and the fights between the mother and daughter turned into physical altercations. Tylar was turning into a different person, she was becoming a monster.

It all started out as what looked like typical teenage rebellion. Tylar embraced the emo and gothic lifestyle by wearing dark and baggy clothes, she had a love of anime and Japanese cartoons, along with everything violent and connected with death. Tylar met her 'Romeo', nineteen year old Steven Colver, at a coffee shop in the popular shopping center of Town Center Shops, where they both frequented. As Tylar was entering her first year of high school, Steven was beginning his first year of college. He was employed as a Shift Lead at Rubio's Mexican Grill. The duo quickly became inseparable. Tylar looked at the older boy as a god and worshiped everything about him. There wasn't anything she wouldn't do for him. The two were in love.

It was in April of 2009, a few weeks after the two had met, that Tylar approached her mother. She convinced her mother that Steven was gay, so that he would be allowed to rent the extra room in their family home. After much resistance from family and friends, Joanne defended the decision by saying that Steven would be helping her make the mortgage payment, as well as help Tylar with her homework. She was described as very strong-willed by her friends and family and didn't let their opinion of others affect her decision to let Steven move in. Joanne didn't suspect a relationship between Steven and her daughter until one day in May, about a month after Steven had moved in. She entered Steven's room and found Steven and Tylar about to engage in a sexual relationship, or had just finished. She found Tylar naked and hiding in Steven's closet, trying to cover herself up. Joanne was understandably upset and demanded that Steven immediately move out. She called two of her male coworkers to come over and assist her. Joanne informed them that she was kicking Steven out of her house and she didn't want to be alone when she did it in case anything were to happen. The male coworkers helped place all of Steven's belongings on the sidewalk and even threatened Steven before he left.

Vinnie Capatano, one of Joanne's coworkers helping her that day, threatened Steven, "If you make contact with Tylar again, either by phone or in person- I am going to hurt you. And I am going to hurt you East Coast style, not West Coast style." It was an act intended to promote intimidation and scare tactics. Steven looked unshaken, which annoyed Capatano even further. His words didn't seem to bother Steven at all.

Joanne was convinced that Steven had committed a crime by sleeping with her underage daughter and made that clear to Steven before he left. She threatened to go to the police and file statutory rape charges if Steven ever came into contact with her daughter again. He didn't take Joanne's words seriously, or the threats of her coworkers. Steven was later found at least twenty more times after this encounter, sneaking into Joanne's house. All Joanne wanted to do was get her daughter away from this older boy that seemed to influence her bad behavior and irrational decisions. Joanne acted as any other mother in this situation would.

Despite the threats, Steven and Tylar continued their love affair and sexual relationship during the day while Joanne was at work and late at night while Joanne was sleeping. Joanne had expressed concern to a few of her coworkers about her daughter's behavior and the boy that seemed able to control and influence her so greatly. It wasn't long until Joanne found out what was going on behind her back and continued to make good on her promise of going to the police. Steven and Tylar vowed to find a way to stay together, no matter the cost. This is the moment the plotting began between the modern day Romeo and Juliet. This was about a month before Joanne Witt was found dead in her home and arrest warrants were issued for her daughter and her daughter's boyfriend.

Joanne Witt located her daughter's diary and handed it over to the police that were handling the statutory rape complaint. The diary clearly outlined the sexual relationship between Tylar Witt and Steven Colver. It explicitly described numerous sexual positions and encounters that the two had shared. There was no mistaking that there was definitely a sexual relationship happening between Steven and Tylar. The detective called to interview Steven about the allegations and Steven claimed that he was worried about Tylar, but their relationship was platonic. He said he considered Tylar as more of a sister figure, than anything else, and he denied any sexual relationship between the two of them. He also admitted that he was scared of this whole situation and he knew she was only fourteen years old. The relationship between Tylar and her mother was volatile and destructive, to say the least, even before she turned in the diary.

Joanne was a loving and attentive single mother that made her daughter, Tylar, the center of her world. However, an incident that took place when Tylar was five years old, prompted an investigation that removed her only daughter from her home. Tylar was placed into foster care for a brief time before Joanne's parents, Norb and Judi Witt could take her in. Tylar lived with them for 6 months while Joanne attended anger management and parenting classes. The incident occurred when Tylar was just five years old after

Joanne had picked her up from daycare. The young girl was screaming in the backseat which was causing Joanne to lose patience very quickly. Joanne reached back and slapped Tylar. The daycare saw the hand shaped mark on Tylar and immediately reported the abuse to CPS, Child Protective Services.

After Tylar was finally able to go back home to her mother, Joanne was afraid to discipline her like she had before. This gave Tylar the opportunity to do whatever she wanted, knowing she could get away with it. Tylar would threaten to call CPS and report her mother again if she didn't get what she wanted. This created many behavioral problems for Tylar and this manifested itself in the violent relationship between the mother and the daughter. Tylar also reported that her mother was a heavy drinker and she would hit and punch Tylar when she was mad. These allegations were never proven. If the violence and abuse had been as severe as Tylar had made it sound, there would have been noticeable marks and bruises on Tylar. They never found any evidence of the abuse she claimed was taking place at the home. There was constant fighting and arguing. Joanne didn't feel comfortable enough start disciplining her daughter again until the few months before that led up to her murder.

The day that Joanne admitted to taking her daughter's diary into the police, was the same night that Joanne and Tylar got into a horrendous fight at home. Tylar felt betrayed by her mother's actions and began throwing objects at her and fighting with her. Tylar called 911 pretending to be Joanne in an attempt to be taken out of the home. She would have rather been in the Juvenile Detention Center than at home with her mother that night. Joanne got onto the phone with dispatch and when they asked her if she was okay, she responded no. Deputies were on their way to the residence. When the police arrived they saw a cut on Joanne's chin and several bruises. Tylar was taken in that night but was released only hours later, after Joanne refused to press charges against her daughter. Joanne was never required to go to the hospital due to her injuries.

Norbert Witt, Tylar's grandfather, claimed that Steven was a bad influence on his granddaughter, and said that he corrupted her by exposing her to sex and heavy narcotics. Steven was known to engage in illegal narcotics such as marijuana, ecstasy, and cocaine.

Norb and Judi Witt owned a luxury RV and had spent the previous two months traveling around the country. They arrived home only days before they received the call that would turn their world upside down. It was Monday when they received a call from Joanne's boss inquiring if they had any idea as to the whereabouts of their daughter. Joanne had an impeccable work history and never missed work without first calling to let them know. So, when Joanne didn't show up or call that Friday, her coworkers began to worry. They stopped by her home that night and knocked on the door, but there was no answer. Nobody seemed to be home. After Joanne didn't show up to work the following Monday either, they knew something was terribly wrong and called the police to report Joanne as missing. After speaking to Joanne's parents and informing them that they had already contacted the police, they raced over to their daughter's house, which was only a few miles away, so they could check themselves. It is there that they met the police. Norb Witt let them into the house to search. The police informed Joanne's parents that she was found upstairs in her room, and she was deceased. There was no sign of a break in or forced entry, there was nothing missing in the home. But where was Tylar? Better yet, where were Tylar and her older boyfriend?

It didn't take the police long to realize that Tylar and Steven had something to do with the cruel and heinous crime in the Witt house. It was only weeks earlier that Joanne had reported Steven to the police and turned in Tylar's diary. She made her feelings about her mother known in the words scrawled throughout the pages. Tylar even plastered her contempt for her mother across her social media sites. She wasn't shy when it came to sharing her feelings and opinion of her mother.

Tylar and Steven went on like normal the days following the murder. They were living the life they wanted now that Tylar's mother wasn't there to get in the middle of it and stop it. They were seen holding hands and kissing, and had seen some of their friends. It was after a night of smoking marijuana and doing lines of cocaine at Steven's father's house that Steven confessed to murdering Joanne and even showed his friend the bloody knife that he was hiding in the car. This friend was Matthew Wildman. Wildman later testified against Steven and told the court that Steven did indeed show him the knife that was used, and he described how the murder happened, and how Steven stood there when he was finished and watched Joanne die. Steven's father came home unexpectedly so they all left the house, with the murder weapon. The murder weapon was never retrieved after their arrest.

The couple had fled to San Francisco, they no longer cared about the consequences because their plan all along was to commit suicide. If they weren't there, they wouldn't have to face the murder charges. According to their logic, that was the only way that they would be able to stay together, without interference, as well as keep Steven out of jail because of the statutory rape charges. They thought the charges would carry a heavy prison sentence and they didn't want to risk separation due to the diary that Joanne had turned into the police earlier.

While in San Francisco, they rented a hotel room and consumed a bazaar mix of fruit loops, cake and rat poison and each had written out suicide notes. The combination of food mixed with the rat poison didn't work, however, and they were arrested shortly after, before they had a second chance to commit suicide. Alongside the food that was found in the hotel room, police also found marijuana, condoms, Steven's work apron and nametag, and the movie 'Donnie Darko' on DVD. They were found changing clothes behind a dumpster at a shopping mall in the area and were arrested by local police and taken in for questioning regarding Joanne Witt's murder.

Once in custody, Tylar refused to admit that she knew her mother was dead and admitted no fault. She asked for a lawyer and for the detectives to go away. The fateful night her mother was brutally murdered was June 11, 2009. Well into the night, after Joanne had finally fallen asleep, Tylar let Steven into the house. He had acquired a chef's knife from his restaurant job at Rubio's. Tylar had grabbed a knife out of the kitchen in her house, and the two proceeded to go upstairs to the bedroom where Joanne Witt was fast asleep. They had each planned to use the knives they had to kill Joanne....together. Tylar claimed that she could not go into the room with Steven. She fell to her knees and covered her ears, while humming to drown out the sound of her mother being stabbed to death. Steven had taken several practice slashes in the air as a warm up before going into Joanne's room and Tylar said this is what prompted her to stay outside of the room. She chose not to go in with Steven. Joanne was stabbed around twenty times. The fatal wound was a gaping slash in her neck. She struggled with her killer and had put her hands up in defense but the wounds were too severe. A bloody knife outline was left on the bed and a book entitled, "How to Parent your Out-Of-Control Teenager, was ironically nestled in the nightstand next to her bed. Tylar and Steven covered Joanne's body with a blanket, turned the air conditioner down in an attempt to preserve the body, and locked up the house and left. They decided to jump the fence instead of having to put the code in to get out. They didn't want anyone to place them there at the time of the murder.

In a suicide letter that Steven had written to his friends, as a kind of apology for what he had done, he said, "Our souls are tainted...We shall be awaiting our fate in the afterworld."

After the news of Joanne's murder got around, a neighbor spoke up about allegedly speaking to Tylar in the park a few months prior. The neighbor had been walking her daughter to the park and claimed she saw a young girl that looked alone, sad, and even angry. The girl was sitting on the swing set with her face toward the ground. She confronted her and asked what was wrong. She said the girl described a bad home life with her mother, and mentioned that her mother liked to drink and would get violent and hurt her, and they would get into a lot of fights. She said the girl seemed really cold and lost in her replies. When asked what Tylar was going to do to stop it the next time it happened she simply replied, "There isn't going to be a next time. Next time it is going to be either her or me." This statement stuck with the neighbor for a long time after. When she realized that the crime scene was a daughter that killed her mother, she finally spoke to police about the conversation in the park. The neighbor was seen on news footage talking to one of the police on the scene, but requested that her name be left out of the media.

Dan Weiner, Steven's attorney, claimed that it was not Steven that committed the murder, it was Tylar. When describing her relationship with Steven, Tylar said, "I trusted him more than I trusted anyone. And I love him more than anybody or anything. If he told me to jump off a bridge and I asked him why and he said just trust me, I would have done it." This shows just how much influence Steven had over Tylar. When neighbors of Steven's were asked to describe him they had only nice things to say.

"He's always been a nice kid as far as I am concerned. If this is true, it is out of character." –Paul Matloff. He also described Steven as a stand-up kid that never played his music too loudly and was always eager to help his neighbors.

Joan Colver, Steven's mother was quoted by reporters as saying, "He would care about others before himself. Steven is the kind of guy who would drive off a cliff or jump in front of a bullet or run into a burning building....for a friend."

When asked why Weiner felt that Steven was being targeted for performing the actual murder instead of Tylar, he didn't really know why. He backed up his defense and Steven's statement of Tylar being the one to murder Joanne Witt, given her past history compared to Steven's.

"He has never hurt anybody, or tried to hurt anybody or threatened to hurt anybody. As contrasted with Tylar who has a very specific history with her mother, and has literally threatened to kill her, to stab her...the very method by which she was ultimately killed!"

Steven had changed his story and said that Joanne was already dead by the time he arrived at the Witt house that night.

"I think realizing the gravity of the situation after being in jail for a while, it took a while before he was willing to confirm, yeah, that she had done it and how she had done it."

Steven said that Tylar stabbed her own mother to death and then called him over to the house after it was done. That is when he claims to have seen the bloody knife. He said that there was blood dripping everywhere, including some spots on Tylar's pants, but there was no evidence of blood droplets being found anywhere else in the house. It was all confined to Joanne's bedroom where she was murdered. The defense claimed that the police failed to look for blood anywhere else except for the primary focus of the house, which was the bedroom. Therefore, there was no evidence available to back up Steven's story. This new story also came about after Steven had already described to his friends how he stabbed his girlfriend's mother to death in her sleep with a butcher knife. Weiner said that Steven was not homicidal, rather suicidal. They claimed that the plan was for Steven to pick up Tylar and they would run off to San Francisco for a few days and then commit suicide together. There was no talk of murdering Joanne. The defense also mentioned that Steven had a clean record, while Tylar's was filled with a history of violence and running away. Despite the new story, Steven's confession to his friend was more than the prosecution needed. He was convicted based on his own words, just as his mother had predicted earlier.

In prosecutor Lisette Suder's words in her opening statement at trial, she described the couple's actions as "a

19 year old man and a 14 year old girl and their love affair that led to the violent almost to the point of sadistic murder of her mother." Tylar was portrayed as an extremely manipulative and brilliant girl. After lying to the detectives when she was first taken into custody and questioned, she finally decided to tell the truth and later passed a polygraph test proving it. She admitted to conspiring with Steven to kill her mother, but also said that it was Steven that committed the actual murder, while she lay in a fetal position outside of the bedroom. All of the evidence found on the scene corroborated Tylar's account of the events from that night. Tylar, in exchange for her testimony against Steven, received a reduced sentence of fifteen years to life for second degree murder. She would be eligible for parole at the age of twenty nine, instead of thirty nine. They were both sentenced at the El Dorado County Superior Court in Placerville.

Joanne Witt's brother, Michael, shared his feelings before sentencing. He was the one that had been responsible for cleaning up his sister's home after the murder. He said he would never be able to get the images of the crime scene photos out of his head.

"I hope and desire that Mr. Colver experiences the worst possible experiences our wonderful prison system can bestow upon him." The judge had tried several times to stop Matthew's rant.

The trial began with Steven still trying to protect Tylar. He didn't want people to accuse his love, Tylar, of being the mother killer. In the beginning stages of his questioning he would ask investigators if they had spoken with Tylar and he inquired about her well-being. He was sympathetic to her situation and just wanted to help her. He thought they were in it together and their love would keep them connected. It ended with the scorned lovers passing the blame to each other. Steven's defense referred to him as an easily manipulated love-struck teen.

Steven's trial lasted for four weeks but the verdict only took four hours to come back. With Tylar's account of the events, the confession Steven made to his friends, and the DNA found underneath Joanne's fingernails that linked the homicide to a male attacker, it all led Steven to a verdict of guilty, for first degree murder. He was sentenced to life in prison without the possibility of parole.

After sentencing, however, Tylar had an interview in which she admitted, "I still have a really hard time being honest. I panic when I get in trouble and the first thing I want to do is lie to get out of it." This statement could potentially be enough to seek an appeal for Steven Colver at a later date. It showed just how dishonest Tylar could be. So if she were able to say this now, what if everything she said in the trial was a lie, despite the polygraph test.

Tylar's psychologist referred to her as a sociopath. Tylar, in trial, said she had three different personalities that were living inside of her. She had her own personality, an angel named Alex, and a demon she referred to as Toby. She claimed her violent actions that led up to this point were because of the demon. Toby would come in times of intense stress. Tylar also described blackouts that she would experience when she was enraged and tried to use the compassion of her dead mother to sway the jury in her favor.

"My mom was not a vicious person and she didn't hold grudges. Even if something horrible like this would have happened, she would have asked for a just punishment. She wouldn't want to see someone suffer for the rest of their lives for a mistake they made when they were being ignorant and stupid."

The following is a letter that Tylar allegedly wrote to her mother before she was murdered. It was Tylar's plan to run away and commit suicide. It was a good bye letter addressed to Joanne.

"As much as you don't think I love you, I do. Not just because I am your daughter but because you are my best friend. Nothing I have ever said to you in anger was ever true. I would never kill you or hate you....but I can't stand to see you so unhappy, but I am growing up and seeing as you don't love me....the person I have become, I see it only fit I do one last thing to make you happy. You want me gone? I am gone."

In Tylar's testimony she admitted the act of violence toward her mother was not a spontaneous decision. It was a decision Steven and Tylar had made after thoroughly discussing their options.

"I was in shock and then I went into a full blown panic attack, hyperventilating, screaming, and shaking." This was in response to Tylar finding out that her mother had turned her diary over to the police in an attempt to build a case against Steven. They came to their own realization that the only way to save Steven from jail was to murder her mother. There was no way they wouldn't file the charges after all the proof was in the diary. They didn't see another way out.

Steven and Tylar concocted this murder plan, afraid that Steven would be sent to prison for a long time because of the statutory rape charges Joanne had filed against him. They didn't want to risk being separated from each other. They saw the murder and subsequent double suicide as a way of staying together. Just like Romeo and Juliet. What they didn't know was that the statutory rape charges only carried a year worth of prison time, if there was any time at all; it was considered a misdemeanor. Instead of a small charge, with little or no prison time, they exchanged a lifetime of freedom for a lifetime of being locked away due to their irrational nature and horrid actions that were compelled by fear. Neither Tylar, nor Steven were able to determine exactly which one of them came up with the idea of killing Joanne. Tylar had been labeled a liar from the very beginning but all of the evidence they had matched with what Tylar had been saying about that night. Everything fit into place and that's why they believed she was finally telling the truth about Steven.

During Tylar's sentencing the judge addressed her directly, "This was a brutal murder. The court has seen no emotion or even remorse for the loss of your mother...I'm sorry for you Miss Witt, because the person who loved you most and without reservation is gone."

Judi Witt had waited a long time before she would go and visit her granddaughter. When she finally set eyes on Tylar she asked how she could have done such a horrible thing. A look of shock plastered across Tylar's face and she responded, "Do you really think I would have been able to do something like this?" When asked if Judi actually believed her, she responded yes.

Not only did they lose their daughter, Judi and Norb Witt also lost their granddaughter. Judi was able to forgive a little easier than Norb. Norb has since written his granddaughter off for killing his daughter. Her actions were inexcusable. She is not the same little girl that they remembered. They said that the Tylar they knew, wasn't the Tylar that killed Joanne. They choose to remember the little girl that they first visited in the hospital after her birth. Tylar was their third grandchild. They recalled the hospital visit after her birth very fondly. They walked in there with a camera and took many pictures, in awe of their own daughter and their new granddaughter. They choose to remember Tylar as the little girl they had watched grow up, not the monster she had become after killing her own mother, not the girl that constantly defied her own mother and threatened her. Not the girl that wrote in her diary about her dream of finding out her mother had died in a car accident. Tylar had lost her way a long time ago. They choose to only remember the good, but revealed that their family was never going to be the same either. Judi and Norb had come to terms with this.

Norb finally decided to go and see Tylar, after the trial. He had refused to go and see her up until this point. When Norb entered the room, Tylar called him Poppa and embraced him. She began sobbing. Norb held onto her tightly and said, after speaking with her, he could see some kind of remorse for what she had done but he still wasn't in the position of being able to forgive her. "It is hard to forgive someone that helped kill your daughter." Norb and Judi do not visit Tylar in prison, but they do say they write to her very often.

In later interviews Tylar finally began showing small signs of remorse for her mother's brutal ending. At one time Tylar had even considered her mom to be her hero and looked at her as not only a mother figure, but also as a father figure, since she never had a real father. Tylar's personalities were all over the place. She would love her mother one day but threaten to kill her the next.

Steven's mother still holds onto the hope of her son's innocence and the possibility of an appeal. She refuses to believe that the boy she knew would be capable of doing something so unforgivable and so violent to someone else.

The tragic death of Joanne Witt and the story of her daughter and her daughter's boyfriend being the murderers shook the community. A violent history with Joanne and her defiance of any kind of authority figures led Tylar into the arms of someone she felt could protect her. The two scorned lovers had a premeditated and thought out plan to kill the object of their resistance. According to their teenage logic, getting rid of Joanne and committing suicide was the only way they could ever be together. Even the most thought out plans tend to backfire, however, and they were very much alive while Joanne was gone. They traded a life of freedom with some restrictions, for a life spent behind bars. They miscalculated the situation and now live to regret it, day after day, year after year.

THE MISSING BEAUTY QUEEN : THE DISAPPEARANCE OF TARA GRINSTEAD

AMANDA DARLING

"I'm an 11th-grade history teacher at Irwin County High school. I also have a cheerleading squad of Junior Varsity cheerleaders. I just completed my first year of teaching, and I love every bit of it." - Tara Grinstead in a 1999 interview.

Tara Grinstead was a beauty pageant winner and high school teacher who strangely disappeared on October 22nd, 2005.

The mystery of her disappearance is as baffling now as it was over ten years ago. Tara was a beautiful woman in a small town and drew the attention of many men. But as investigators peeled back the onion on her life, they discovered that she had a complex personal life, one with many lovers and layers of relationship any one of whom may have sought to do her harm out of jealousy.

Investigators have pieced together the timeline of her activities prior to her disappearance. But the missing piece lies sometime during the night of October 22nd, 2005, when someone abducted Tara Grinstead and she would never be seen again.

What happened to Tara Grinstead?

EARLY LIFE

Tara was born on November 14th, 1974 to Faye and Billy Grinstead. She grew up in Hawkinsville, Georgia and was a popular cheerleader in high school as well as a diligent student. Her parents would divorce and her father would remarry a woman named Connie to whom Tara grew close to as well.

Tara loved animals, singing and going to church as a kid.

One cannot look upon pictures and video of Tara and not remark that she had a striking beauty. Graced with a voluptuous figure and long black hair, she had the ability to light up any room she walked into. She would eventually compete in beauty pageants, falling in love with the preparation, competition, and glamor of the activity.

"She had been into so many (pageants) that I had lost count," Connie Grinstead said.

Tara meticulously prepared for the pageants, remaining physically fit, taking speech lessons and learning how to sing. She would also graduate from Middle Georgia College and become a teacher at Irwin County High School in Ocilla. She would teach history to 11th graders but not give up on her pageant hopes.

In 1999, she would achieve the first step in her dream to enter the Miss USA contest, when she would win the local title of Miss Tifton.

This victory would allow her to compete in the Miss Georgia pageant. She would also receive scholarship winnings that she would use to help pay for her continuing college education.

"It was, for her, more than a dream come true," Tara's best friend Maria Hulett said. "It was the chance for her to be really proud of herself."

Footage of Tara during the Georgia pageant showed her to be an exuberant woman with a zest for life. She loved to exercise, drink Diet Coke with grenadine, collect Barbies and listening to 80s music like Bon Jovi. She had an infectious smile and played to the camera as she showed off her yellow business suit that she would wear for the pageant interview.

"Why did you pick yellow?" the reporter asked.

"Because it shows that I'm a happy person," Tara said.

With her pageant days behind her, Tara would earn a master's degree in education from Valdosta State University.

"She wanted to be a principal," her friend Oshja Anderson said. "She was well on her way."

Always seeking to improve herself, Tara would teach classes during the day and go to graduate school at night. She also held down a part-time job selling cosmetics at the local department store. By 2005, she had applied for a doctoral program in history and would occasionally fill in as the assistant principal.

"On the surface," forensic psychiatrist Orange said. "Tara's life looked to be a stellar one. She had a bright future in academia and during her pageant days, she learned to put forward the best appearance. But what lurked underneath in her personal life is the mystery."

MARCUS HARPER

At the heart of Tara's disappearance is figuring out the type of relationships she had with the numerous men in her life. She worked as a teacher, went to night school and worked the cosmetics counter at a department store. Outgoing and bubbly, she didn't have the personality type to reject anyone out of hand. She attracted men and had many suitors.

She did have a longtime boyfriend in Marcus Harper.

Harper was an Ocilla police officer who would later become an Army Ranger. Both of Tara's parents liked him as they both expressed the fact that he always remained respectful of them. They have consistently maintained that they never witnessed Harper treating Tara with disrespect.

Tara, however, had expressed to her sister that she was afraid of Marcus.

"She said she was afraid of him," Tara's sister Anita said. "What he had gone through with the Ranger training. He was capable of anything."

"Marcus was a strong Alpha-male type," Orange said. "A cop and an Army Ranger. Tara was rumored to have dated another cop as well but she didn't appear to have a type. From what we can gather, she dated a slew of men from older to younger, and from different walks of life."

About a year prior to her disappearance, Tara had broken up with Marcus. She had given him an ultimatum and wanted to be married. He did not want marriage but wanted to remain committed. The relationship would turn sour at that point.

Tara would begin to date other people. She was in a car with a romantic suitor named Rhett Roberts who was the son of her landlord.

Marcus spotted the couple and would go ballistic, shouting obscenities at Tara.

Despite this angry confrontation, Tara would maintain ties with Marcus. In late July or early August of 2005 they would go to St. Augustine on a beach trip. After their date, Tara would confide to a friend that she was concerned about Marcus's temper.

Marcus would then be deployed back to Iraq a few weeks later. Tara would write the Army Ranger a letter in which she effectively ended their relationship.

According to Marcus, however, their relationship didn't come to a close until October of 2005. He had returned from the Middle East and called Tara to tell her that their relationship was over. Tara was at work and became so distraught that had to pull over to the side of the road. She called a friend who came and took her home. The next day, Tara would call off sick from her teaching job in order to "take a mental health day."

There was a rumor that a cop from a neighboring town, Heath Dykes, came to visit Tara at her school shortly afterward.

"These behaviors certainly show some mental fragilities on the parts of both Tara and Marcus," Orange said. "From what we can gather, it looked like an off-and-on style relationship with a few other romantic partners thrown in for good measure. It is unclear as to who was chasing who at various points of their relationship. If we are to believe Marcus, then she was chasing him. If we are to believe Tara's sister, then she was afraid of him. Why would you chase a man that you were afraid of? Something is not right here."

A few days later, Tara and Marcus would have another "heated argument" which she would tell one of her friends at her night class as well as another friend the next day while she had lunch.

According to Marcus, the argument centered around him breaking up with her. But Tara's sister Anita Gattis had a different story.

"They had a very bad argument," Anita said. "Several days before she went missing, concerning an 18-year-old that he was dating. My sister did not think that (the 18-year-old's) parents would approve of a 30-year-old dating an-18-year-old. I'm told that she threatened to tell the parents and they had a very heated argument over this."

Marcus said the argument was about something else entirely. He stated that she begged him not to end their relationship.

"She wanted me back and all," Marcus said. "And I said, 'I've started shopping outside of Ocilla, I think you need to do the same. Everybody in this town is connected to us one way or another."

"She approached me crying," Harper said as he repeated the same story on Greta Van Susteren's TV show. "She was very irrational, and she told me that if she found out I was dating someone, she would commit suicide."

But Tara's friend Osjha disputes the fact that Tara would do or say something like that.

"She's never said anything remotely similar to me ever any time."

Law enforcement authorities don't believe Tara committed suicide as she would have to go to extreme lengths to hide her own body and would have no motive to do so.

"There are a couple of contradictory things at play here," Orange said. "Tara was rumored to have dated some of her students so it would be hypocritical of her to criticize Marcus for dating someone in their teens. And it also doesn't make sense for her to come to Marcus' home begging to get back together. She had her share of suitors, some coming from out of town. She was a beautiful woman and she had options."

To her family's dismay, both the authorities and press would place Tara's life under a microscope. They had discovered that she had "several romantic relationships that occurred in relative proximity to one another."

"There was more rumors and innuendo," Orange said. "There were rumors that she was dating Rhett Roberts, her landlord's son. Rumors that she was dating one of her teenage students. Rumors that she was dating Heath Dyke, a police officer from another county. Even her own brother-in-law, Larry Gattis, was rumored to have an affair with Tara."

Both Larry and Tara's sisters are physicians. Larry specializes in geriatric medicine with only 3.3 out of 5-star reviews on Healthgrades. He was interrogated by investigators and expressed his outrage at the questions they were asking. One question was that if he had an affair with Tara and his response was judged by the polygraph as "deceptive."

ALL THAT AND A STALKER TOO...

Tara would have a stalker in a former student named Anthony Vickers. Friends recalled that Tara had taken special care to tutor Vickers but she later realized that the young man was "unstable."

"He was just kind of a troubled kid and that would be her nature," Osjha said.

Vickers was obsessed with his beauty queen teacher and claimed to have had a romantic relationship with her.

"She talked about the fact that he would call and he would rely on her and she knew it was getting too much for her," a friend named Maria said. "I just kept telling her, 'You know Tara, something's wrong."

Vickers was two years out of high school when he came to Tara's house and demanded to be let in. He pounded on the door until she called the police. Vickers resisted arrest but charges were later dropped and no restraining orders were ever filed.

The Vickers incident wasn't the only occasion that the former beauty pageant winner was being stalked. There was an incident where someone would call her home and make threats. The call was traced and it was determined to be a student in her homeroom who was promptly removed from the class.

THE NIGHT OF...

Before the night of her disappearance, Tara had enjoyed the company of her friend Dana and some teenage girls as they readied for the "Miss Georgia Sweet Potato" pageant. Her friend remembered

Tara as being in a great mood, helping out the girls with their hair and makeup. She would attend the pageant where she served as a backstage coach. Later that evening, she went to the house of a neighbor before going to a barbecue a few blocks from her home . Police believe that she had remained at the barbecue until 11 pm when she left to go home. They would find the clothes she wore at the cookout on her bedroom floor which indicated to police that she had, in fact, returned home.

From that point on, police "have no idea" what happened to Tara.

On October 24th, 2005, Tara did not show up to teach her class. Her colleagues called the police who showed up at her residence to do a welfare check. They would find her white Mitsubishi parked in the garage, unlocked. Upon entering her home, police found a business card lodged in her door.

There appeared to be no sign of forced entry. Searching through the house, police found her cell phone plugged into her charger. Her purse and keys could not be found.

Strangely, the clothes she wore the night before were piled on the bedroom floor.

Investigators found it odd that the car door was unlocked and that the car seat was pushed back. Tara was petite at only five-foot-three and would have kept the seat much closer to the steering wheel. They found an envelope of cash (one hundred dollars) on her dashboard while both her dog and cat were inside. Tara's sister said that she was an animal lover who would never just abandon her pets.

Something was wrong...

The police immediately called the Georgia Bureau of Investigation as the lacked the resources to pursue this kind of crime.

Taking over the case, the GBI believed that Tara may have left with someone that she knew, given the lack of a forced entry and the fact that only her purse and keys were missing. Neighbors did not report hearing any screaming at night.

Her disappearance shocked the small and close-knit community. To a person, Tara was described as someone who had a great personality, loved by faculty and students alike. Nothing in her professional life would suggest that she had any enemies.

Volunteers from the community immediately went to work. Irwin County students, teachers, and other townsfolk searched the area and put out flyers.

"Missing. Tara Grinstead. $20,000 Reward."

ROUNDING UP THE SUSPECTS

Longtime boyfriend Marcus Harper was one of the first to be questioned. He came with a ready-made alibi for the night of Tara's disappearance.

Marcus was seen at a bar with friends then went on a 'ride-along' with a former partner on the local police force. His whereabouts was "essentially substantiated" according to authorities.

Former student/stalker Anthony Vickers was questioned but later ruled out as a suspect. Like the others, however, he could not account for the entire thirty-four hour period when Tara was last seen and reported missing.

"Vickers is probably the only one I would rule out," Orange said. "This disappearance was too clean. Vickers was a disturbed twenty-year-old man with a crush. He would not have the emotional wherewithal or the knowledge to pull off a crime with no clues. But someone with law enforcement or medical training could."

But who left the business card behind at her door?

The card was left by Heath Dykes, a married Perry police officer with two children. He was from the next town over and had known Tara since high school.

Neighbors would tell investigators that he visited Tara's house often. It is unclear what their relationship was (outside of the obvious innuendo and rumors).

Still, he had left close to two dozen messages on Tara's answering message on the weekend she went missing.

There is small-town gossip that the two were having an affair. Local witnesses have confirmed that they saw his wife throw his clothes out on the front lawn. The content of the messages he left have not been made public but the rumors were that he was telling her "he was sorry" and that he "loved her."

What is clear is that he did call Tara's mother from the front yard and ask if she knew where Tara was and if she was alright.

Heath Dykes was the last known person at Tara's home that night as he arrived a little after midnight.

"There are simply too many secrets here," Orange said. "Something was clearly going on in Heath's mind in order for him to call Tara that many times over the course of one evening. One rumor is that they were having an affair and that she was going to tell his wife. So he was calling her in a desperate attempt to stop her from doing that. Another possibility was that she was calling him for help and he was returning her calls. His involvement led to a lot of outlandish speculation, one of which was that Heath knew that a hit man was coming for Tara and that he was calling to make sure that she was okay."

"I think the fact that she was beautiful and other people paid attention to her would obviously make some people jealous," Tara's friend Maria said. "I think she was afraid of the possibility of someone hurting her from being angry at her, having reactions to her dating people."

Numerous men were rounded up and questioned, there was Jim Perry who dated Tara years earlier, Rhett Roberts, Marcus Harper, Anthony Vickers, and Eric Cook among others.

Another unsubstantiated rumor that Tara was involved with another student named Eric Cook. A friend of his had made mention of their affair in an Internet forum post where he stated that everyone knew that they were "messing around." He also said that the police didn't make the information public out of respect for Tara's family as she dated around quite a bit. An alleged friend of Cook disputed the rumor on the forum, however. Cook would later die in a car accident.

A neighbor, Joe Poirier lived with his wife and was rumored to have been "obsessed" with Tara. The older couple admitted to "looking out for Tara" and they were fond of her. He was seen pouring concrete near his home the day after she disappeared.

Another person of interest was Larry Gattis, the brother-in-law of Tara. He was brought in for questioning after the disappearance. It would later be revealed that he had been asked if he had an affair with Tara.

Larry answered 'no.'

The polygraph machine marked it as a 'deceptive answer.'

48 HOURS

In 2008, Tara's case would be featured on the CBS News show "48 Hours Mystery." The show would illustrate the parallels between Tara's case and the disappearance of Jennifer Kesse who would go missing in Orlando, Florida three months later. The GBI would also reveal during the broadcast that they had found a latex glove in Tara's yard just a few feet away from her front porch.

The GBI forensic team would analyze the DNA left in the glove and determine that it was a man's DNA, they just do not know who it belongs to. They would compare the DNA samples of the numerous men who were associated with or knew Tara but none of them have matched.

The DNA has also been entered into the Georgia and national databases but no match has been made to date.

"The glove may be a red herring," Orange said. "Whoever entered the home left nothing behind, no prints, DNA, nothing. So it was obviously someone who knew exactly what they were doing. They wanted to harm Tara."

A HOAX AND FALSE TIPS

In February of 2009, a man calling himself the "Catch Me Killer" began posting videos boasting that he had murdered sixteen women. One of the women he described had a close resemblance to Tara Grinstead. The man producing the video digitally obscured his face and voice but police eventually identified the culprit as twenty-seven-year-old Andrew Haley.

Haley performed the videos as part of a bizarre hoax and was eliminated as a possible suspect.

Investigator Gary Rothwell has expressed his lament at how the rumors and speculation have caused unfair stress to many who have been already tried in the public eye. "Irresponsible public accusations have been made about them, and they have no way to respond or defend themselves. And it's frustrating that we don't have evidence to rule anyone in or out."

Rothwell admits, however, that he has information that has not been released.

In February of 2015, authorities acted on a tip which led them to drain a pond in Fitzgerald, Georgia.

They didn't go into details as to what the specifics of the tip were. The pond would be drained and nothing would be found.

ALIBIS

Police have alibis from all the men who knew Tara Grinstead but no one has been ruled out because no one can account for the full thirty-four hour period.

Rhett Reynolds stated he went to sleep after the cookout. Joe Poirier was with his wife next door.

The most elaborate alibi, however, came from Marcus Harper.

Again, Marcus was in a local bar and a friend of Tara's had spotted him there. She would call Tara at around 10:15 and 10:30 to tell Tara that Marcus was there.

After 1 am, Marcus left the bar and went to look for his police officer friend, Sgt. Sean Fletcher. Fletcher was on duty that night.

Fletcher knew Tara as well. Ironically, he was one of the officers who arrived at Tara's house when Anthony Vickers, Tara's former student, was banging on her door.

There were rumors that Tara didn't like Fletcher because he had told Harper that Tara was entertaining Heath Dykes at her home.

Fletcher would deny that speculation.

"What we can extrapolate from this scenario was that Vickers was angry that his crush, Tara, was with another man," Orange said. "So he goes to her home and demands that she talk to him. He's young, twenty-years-old, and doesn't understand why she would do this to him. He is then arrested by Fletcher who relays what Tara is doing to Marcus, a man that Tara is wary about because of his temper. So now we have more than just a love triangle, it is a love octagon, with numerous men vying for and getting jealous over the attention of Tara."

At around 1:49 am, Fletcher received a call from dispatch informing him that Marcus Harper was looking for him. The two met up and walked Fletcher's beat, checking doors in downtown Ocilla.

Around 2:45, Fletcher was dispatch to a home where a mentally unbalanced man, Bennie Merritt, had stumbled into a home and refused to leave. Marcus would join Fletcher on the call as did two other officers. Merritt, however, was gone from the premises.

Minutes later, they began to search for Merritt who was also a neighbor of Tara's. The drunken Merritt would accost the cashier at the local gas station then be apprehended. Both Fletcher and Harper had responded to the call at the gas station and by the time they were done it was 4:28 am.

Marcus then headed home.

Investigators would later be able to corroborate these details with multiple witnesses, including Merritt, who was scrutinized as a possible suspect in the kidnapping as well.

Marcus Harper, however, has not been ruled out as a potential person of interest in the case.

"Marcus's alibi is too perfect," GBI investigator Maurice Godwin said.

Both Larry and Anita Gattis believe that Marcus is the top suspect.

"He had the motive," Tara's sister said. "And the training."

The insinuation would draw the ire of Marcus who became upset that Anita consistently brought up his military and police training. He continues to deny any involvement in Tara's disappearance.

"I don't wanna hurt any innocent civilian much less someone I spent five and a half years of my life with."

"What is clear is that there isn't a whole lot forthcoming about Tara's personal life to draw the conclusions we need to about who is the most probable suspect," Orange said. "Like in the Natalee Holloway case, the sexual activity of the woman in question is kept hidden. If her background reveals that she was a promiscuous woman, there will e less sympathy and urgency to solve the crime. That is one of the more striking aspects of the case, aside from Tara's vanishing, is the cover-up of Tara's personal life in order to protect her reputation."

UNSOLVABLE CASE?

Tara Grinstead's case is still being investigated. The GBI reports that they receive numerous leads per day, most of which are false.

Her body has never been found but her impact on the lives of those around her and her students will never be forgotten.

"I'm so sorry to hear about what happened to Miss Grinstead," said Christine Kang, a South Korean exchange student from Grinstead's class. "She is so caring and giving to her students. I am sure she will come home soon safely. I will pray for her every night."

MURDER IN TEXAS : THE TRUE STORY OF RHONDA JOHNSON & SHARON SHAW

JAMIE FOSTER

Rhonda Johnson and Sharon Shaw were two teenage girls murdered in 1971. But despite having had their lives taken so long ago, their case is still not satisfactorily solved. It's a story that involves not just two girls being murdered so young, but a potentially innocent man imprisoned for over twenty years, a corrupt police force, a serial killer, and perhaps the wider context of the Texas Killing Fields murders.

The story of the twists and turns involved in finding justice for the two girls continues on until today. Michael Lloyd Self, the man who some believe to have been wrongly imprisoned for the murder of the two girls, has since died in prison of cancer. Because of his passing, and the difficulty that investigators have found in unearthing new evidence, it seemed unlikely that the full story will ever come out.

But not long ago, a revelation and a startling confession have brought Johnson and Shaw's murders back into the limelight. Perhaps, at last, their families can discover the truth of their real killers.

Who were Rhonda Renee Johnson and Sharon Shaw?

Sharon Lynn Shaw was born in Mobile, Alabama to Hoyt Shaw and Mary Ann Collins on August 11th, 1957. Rhonda was born in Houston, Texas to Charles Johnson Sr. and Betty Huey on December 16th, 1956. Not much is known of their early lives, although by 1971 they were living next to one another in Webster, Texas, and were good friends.

Both girls had finished with school for the year and were enjoying their time off together. The day of their disappearance began like many others that summer, with a day out on a pleasant morning. It was August 4th, 1971 and Johnson and Shaw wanted to take a day trip to Galveston, to Wix Ski School, and to visit Doug's Surf and Dive Shop which was nearby. The area also had a Dairy Queen and a popular swimming school, making it very popular with the teenagers of the surrounding area. Given that it was summer, the girls would most likely have preferred to stay all day, but had promised their parents that they would be home by 1pm.

They hitched a ride with a family friend, who took them on the 30 mile journey to Galveston. Unfortunately for the girls' parents, that morning would be the last that they would ever see of their children.

The afternoon came and went, and the girls didn't call home to explain their absence. After they missed dinner that night, their parents began to call their friends to see if they'd heard from them, and called the neighbor who had given them a ride. None of their friends had heard a thing, and the last their neighbor had seen was when the girls had been dropped off at the skiing school and surf club. The girls were soon reported missing by their parents, who went in person to the local police department.

According to Raymond Wix, the owner of Wix Ski School, the girls didn't stay long there that day. In conversation with the Webster Police Department, he had told them that they had headed off after being told that the ski boats weren't running that day due to choppy waters. That was the last that we can say with certainty about the girls' day.

It was in August that the pair crossed paths with the man who would end their lives, but it wasn't until the beginning of 1972 that the girls' bodies were found. Just after the New Year, two young men went fishing near Webster, Texas, their hometown. They came across a skull floating in the marsh, and one of the men wrapped it up in a towel, stowed it away and took it home. After sharing their find with the Harris County Sherriff, the skull was eventually identified as belonging to the missing Rhonda Johnson.

This triggered a large scale search of Taylor Lake and the Bayou, which despite its size took until February 17th to find any more evidence. That day, another skull was found in a nearby drainage ditch, and soon more bones were found. They were identified as belonging to both girls.

Michael Lloyd Self tried and convicted

While the girls' bodies were discovered in early January, it was only in late May the same year that progress began on their case. The city council hired a new police chief that month, Don Morris, who brought with him a new assistant chief, Tommy Deal. Eager that they be seen to be doing something on such a large crime for a small town, the pair acted on a tip they'd received about local man Michael Lloyd Self.

Self was, admittedly, a sex offender known locally who had already been arrested multiple times in 'Peeping Tom' incidents. It was Morris and Deal themselves who visited Self at his place of work, a gas station, where Self was working night shifts at the time. They questioned him on the topic of the 'two girls'- the officers, of course, referring to Johnson and Shaw. Self, however, believed them to mean his estranged wife and new girlfriend, and having been confused went to the police station later that day to clear the matter.

Upon his arrival, he was again questioned about Johnson and Shaw, this time being shown their photographs and interrogated on his connection to them. Self admitted to recognising them, and unfortunately for him, that seemed to be enough evidence for the new chief: he was arrested then and there on the charge of their murders.

Since he was now officially detained at the station- he had, after all, only arrived voluntarily that morning- Self's interrogation could now begin in earnest. Morris and Deal claimed that their suspicions rested on evidence that they had obtained, and urged him to confess. According to Jerry Mitchell, another officer at the police station that day, Self appeared calm and rational throughout the early stages of his questioning, clearly expecting any second that the officers would realise they had the wrong man.

He continued to deny the crimes as the morning wore on, but according to Self, the interrogations became continually more threatening and violent. Morris held him up against the wall, jabbed him with his nightstick, and even threatened to shoot him were he to carry on denying the crimes. Finally, Self had had enough: he wrote out his confession. He would later claim that Morris told him what to write, even forcing him to rewrite his confession several times over, a claim echoed once more by Jerry Mitchell.

During his time in court, Michael claimed that his confession had been forced out of him by the two officers interrogating him. These concerns were quickly dismissed, since after all, which murderer doesn't deny the charges against them?

Self's Confession: Details and Inconsistencies

It is easy to see why a jury or a prosecutor might be taken in by the confession, were they to consider the case 'open and shut' and not give it enough thought. It is particularly detailed with regards to the murders. Self first describes how he picked up Rhonda as he saw her walking along the road, turning around to pick her up in his car. They then drove to the Nassau Bay Yacht Club, where Rhonda found her friend Sharon. He claimed that he provided them with beer, offered them marijuana which they declined, and drove around the Clear Lake area 'feel[ing] good and getting loud.'

As the night wore on, Self's version of events is that Sharon had been hanging out of the window 'hollering at everybody and shooting peace signs at them' as he drove. Since neither of the girls wanted to go home, he claimed they went down to Clear Lake where he tried to assault Rhonda, which she rejected. Since Sharon was out of the car, Self continued assaulting her, and at her continued protests he became angry and hit both Sharon and Rhonda over the head with a Coke bottle repeatedly until they were both unconscious.

He goes on to describe how he drove the girls to an abandoned, dead end road, stripped them of their clothes and dumped their bodies in the Bayou.

Reading back the confession that Self may or may not have been forced to write, it is at least easy to spot several glaring, obvious mistakes. Perhaps the worst is that according to his confession, Self disposed of the girls' bodies more than twenty miles from where they were actually found. Both of the girls were found with their clothes on, not stripped as Self had claimed. Even the method by which he confessed to having murdered Johnson and Shaw was incorrect according to the coroner's report, with Self claiming to have strangled the girls, but their bodies showing no such marks.

Moreover, Sharon's family dispute the confession since it mentions Self picking up the young girl from her family home, which they deny. The confession also states that Self and the two girls were in Webster at 9pm, whereas eyewitnesses disagree and place the two girls- alone- in Galveston instead. The written confession is even further discredited by Self's later verbal confessions, which contradict several key points. For instance, Self repeated his claim during a polygraph test taken three days after his initial arrest that he stripped the girls before dumping their bodies, when they were in fact found with their clothes on.

The story only continues to get stranger. Two weeks after Self was first arrested, while the officers were still building the case against him, he was actually taken from jail by two deputies. They had told Self that they were going to buy him dinner. In fact, they took him out of town to the locations which Self had mentioned in his confessions to take pictures of him as a sort of third and final confession. These photos were even presented in court as evidence.

This episode is mentioned in the court records of Self's appeal. There, the scene is painted as Self agreeing to show the two deputies the various locations involved in the murder. First, the group went to the Sizzler Steak House, where Self said he picked up Rhonda (contradicting his claim that he had picked her up on El Camino Real, a nearby street, where she had been walking). According to this testimony, after picking up Sharon they then went to a Jack in the Box restaurant. The fact that this confession had been so different to his previous one, however, did not constitute enough of a problem for either confession to be inadmissible according to the court records of Self's appeal case.

Time passes by

After Self's conviction, justice did appear to have been done. Trust in the police was higher than it is today; if a man had been arrested, tried, and convicted of a crime then the case was, quite simply, closed. Self, for his part, never gave in. He continually appealed the case and applied for parole, beginning taking the case to an appeals court just a year after his first imprisonment.

According to the court records, Self complained on several grounds. First, he claimed that the evidence presented at his first trial was 'insufficient to sustain his conviction', mostly due to his claim that his confession was forced, but also because the photos taken at the various locations relevant to the case shouldn't have been admitted as evidence.

Unfortunately, each time Self applied for parole, or put his case up for appeal, he was unsuccessful. In the eyes of the law there was little reason to overturn the ruling. Self's first confession did contain some errors, but was also correct on several points, particularly that the bodies were disposed of and found in water. At appeal, the judge decided that enough of the confession corroborated with material evidence to uphold the previous verdict.

While Self's protests had been dismissed, the case still seemed to some to be too flimsy to have justified the certainty of a seventy year sentence. Like many similar cases before his, Self's case was eventually dramatized as part of the TV show, Unresolved Mysteries. David Coburn, a local investigator interviewed in the episode, actually backed up Self's story of Morris' mistreatment of him during his interrogation. Coburn claimed that he had seen Morris' brutality first hand during another interrogation the year before. The show raised the same questions as Self had done, but of course left it to the viewer to decide as to whether he truly was guilty or not.

Morris and Deal's Motives: The Texas Killing Fields

The show also raised the question of why, exactly, Morris and Deal had been so eager to arrest Self on such little evidence. In all of their efforts to extract repeated confessions from the defendant, it certainly seemed that they must have had their reasons. First, Self was well known locally for his sexual misdemeanors. For the city, it would make their lives a lot easier to finally put Self away for a longer sentence. It also made sense for the new chief to make it obvious that he was hard on crime. A new chief not addressing one of the largest and most shocking cases in Webster history would certainly give a bad first impression.

Last, but certainly not least, is the fact that the area had seen an unnaturally large number of murders from the start of the 1970s, which we today call the Texas Killing Fields murders. If Johnson and Shaw really were victims of the same serial killer as the other murders in the area, they were some of the very first to be killed. However, by the time they were discovered, five other girls' bodies had been found in the local area.

Whether law enforcement at the time would have recognised that these murders were perhaps the work of a repeat killer, they would at least have been aware of the spate of local killings, and been desperate to pin the crime on somebody. This, perhaps, was part of the reason why Morris and Deal were more eager than they should have been to try to pin those crimes on Self. At the very least, newspaper clippings from the time of the investigation reveal the public concern over previous missing persons' cases, as well as the deaths of many other young girls from the area. In a copy of The Odessa American from June 10th 1970, the author reveals that Self was suspected to perhaps have had a hand in the many other recent local murders.

The two girls were far from the last victims, however, as the Texas Killing Fields murders continued through the 1980s and 1990s, some even coming after the turn of the century. Almost every victim has been between the ages of 12 and 17, and every victim has been a young girl or woman. In total, at least 30 bodies have been found all within a 25 acre area just off I-45. Even aside from the discovered bodies, many more local girls have gone missing and are featured on websites like The Charley Project, a site dedicated to tracking down missing persons. All of this has led some to believe that the murders must be the work of a serial killer.

They certainly fit the bill: all around the same area, the vast majority of the victims fitting the same description, and a relatively steady pace of killings through the years all suggest the work of one lone actor. The only real argument against the idea is the fact that the killer must somehow have remained at large for so long, despite leaving such an obvious trail. If the murder of Johnson and Shaw really were part of the Texas Killing Fields murders- and given that the murders were often of pairs of young girls around their age, it would seem very likely- then Self could not have been their killer, since the murders continued for long after he was incarcerated.

A Twist in the Tale

Whether the Texas Killing Fields murders were the acts of a lone serial killer, or how he must be innocent if Johnson and Shaw were two victims of that same killer, was irrelevant to Michael Lloyd Self. Despite all of his protestations, appeals, and parole hearings, he remained in prison. It was only in 1998 that any development in this seemingly long-dead case came about. Edward Harold Bell was already in prison, after a manhunt that spanned the globe. He had been on the run since 1978, after the attempted assault of a group of children and the murder of a Marine, Larry Dickens, who had attempted to intervene.

The murder was especially brutal. It had taken place in a normal, suburban street; Bell had been coasting around in his car, searching for girls. Finding a group of young teenagers, he had stopped his car and jumped out, not wearing anything below the waist. Dickens, a local resident, noticed what was happening and attempted to intervene. Unfortunately for him, Dickens didn't like being interrupted.

He went back to his car, picked up a pistol and began shooting. Larry struggled back to the garage, where his mother had been watching the scene, and collapsed in her arms. Bell didn't stop shooting. When he ran out of bullets in his pistol, he went back to his truck to exchange it for his rifle, and carried on.

Bell would have been guaranteed life in prison for the brutal murder, but skipped bail and went on the run for 15 years. In 1984 he be was identified as part of a failed burglary in Texas, but still managed to avoid the police before finally being tracked down in Panama in 1993. Upon his eventual capture, he was finally convicted of the murder of Dickens and received 70 years in prison. Bell's murder of Dickens, too, was featured on Unresolved Mysteries; curiously, Matthew McConaughey caught his first big break on TV playing the role of Larry.

His connection to the Johnson and Shaw case was completely unknown before he confessed not just to their murders, but to the murder of eleven girls in total in the 1970s. The frankly disturbing letters were sent to prosecutors for both Harris County and Galveston County way back in 1998, but were kept under wraps until 2011. The letters initially claimed a tally of seven lives, but in interviews with the Houston Chronicle after their publication admitted to the total of eleven murders. In them, he claimed to have been a part of a government brainwashing program that forced him to assault, rape, and kill young girls.

Who Was Edward Harold Bell?

According to the Houston Chronicle, Bell had a 'normal' early life, 'even exemplary'. A boy scout who went on to earn a degree from Texas A&M, he made his living first as a licensed diver- where he met his wife- before settling as a travelling pharmaceutical salesman in West Texas. On the surface, he seemed like a normal man, with a normal job, and a happy wife and family.

According to Bell himself, however, his childhood was not idyllic. His family were always on the move since his father worked as a gauger at small oil fields across Texas, earning plenty of money to provide for his wife and son but forcing them to live an itinerant lifestyle. Not just this, but Bell also claimed that his father was excessively violent towards his family: in Bell's own words, 'My father thought if he beat you real bad, it would send chemicals into your bloodstream.' Bell fathered three children of his own over the years- but what his family didn't know was that he was leading a sordid double life.

Bell's crimes began much the same way as Self's had done: Bell progressed from peeping tom incidents, to masturbating in public and exposing himself to girls around Texas. According to the Chronicle, he was apprehended committing public indecencies at least twelve times, from Lubbock to Houston; his targets, teenage girls, often in pairs, but always unaccompanied by adults. More often than not, he managed to avoid prosecution or arrest for his actions. He began- at least, he was first caught- in 1968, exposing himself to teenage girls in the town of Sudan. Police and court records show that he continued on and off until at least 1978, the year he murdered Larry Dickens for interrupting an episode of his flashing.

Bell was in and out of mental institutions for a large part of that decade, on referral from court. He somehow didn't receive a single jail sentence for any of his sexual crimes, something which most likely wouldn't happen today. If he had been appropriately dealt with by the police for his previous crimes, the life of Larry Dickens could have been saved. In fairness to the police, however, his violent outburst was entirely unprecedented.

What Happened Next?

It would seem that at last, justice could have been done. Through all the years, Self had maintained his innocence, continued to claim that his confession had been forced, and that despite knowing the girls he had not been involved in their murders. Bell was a known murderer, already in prison, and provided remarkably accurate details with relevance to several missing persons cases in his letters. It would seem that given this detail, and Bell's prior crimes, that his confessions would force prosecutors to re-open the case and for Self's version of events, perhaps, to be reheard and finally believed.

All of this was not to be. As is so often the case with decades-old missing persons cases- in particular cases that seemed as closed as this- the new evidence wasn't treated with the interest it should have been. Astonishingly, Galveston County refused to present the letters to a jury for their consideration, and even worse, Harris County actually lost the letters altogether. Self remained in prison, unaware that a confession had even been made.

One of the prosecutors for Galveston County stated to the Houston Chronicle that he "...didn't believe we had sufficient evidence that we could proceed to grand jury with, and without getting into specifics, that's the decision that had to be made, no matter the temptations to proceed otherwise ... It wasn't for a lack of effort." In fairness to the prosecutors, the evidence to reopen a case of murder- particularly one that already, in the eyes of the law, has been settled- has to be very compelling, and perhaps the confession of a man known to be mentally unstable is not enough. After all, serial killers have been known to confess to crimes they may not have committed to gain infamy, or recapture the spotlight long after their conviction.

It was only two years later that Michael Lloyd Self died in prison, of cancer. If he really was innocent- and on the balance of probabilities, it seems that he may have been- then he will never see justice for his unlawful incarceration, which lasted a total twenty seven years before his death.

As for Bell, he remains in prison. He received 70 years for the inexplicably brutal murder of Larry Dickens, and so any sentence received for the murders of Johnson and Shaw- not to mention the other girls he claimed to have killed in the same letters- would be irrelevant. Bell was in his late 70s at the time of writing, and will die in prison.

The Johnson and Shaw cases are still, officially, the crimes of Michael Lloyd Self, and the case remains closed. Since Bell's letters were received by county prosecutors, no new evidence has come to light; the letters and accompanying information were not considered enough to reopen the case then, and aren't considered enough now. And due to Bell's refusal to co-operate with police, it seems unlikely that any new information on his potential part in the murders will ever be revealed.

THE DISAPPEARANCE OF KELSIE SCHELLING

ANA BENSON

Every time a woman goes missing or is found murdered, the police usually takes a closer look at their spouses or boyfriends. It is a standard procedure, especially if there were indications that they were in a troubled relationship. The disappearance of Kelsie Schelling is one of the biggest mysteries in Colorado. This young pregnant woman was last seen in February of 2013 and the case is still open to this day.

However, Kelsie's family was quite disappointed at the lack of interest by the police to investigate her then-boyfriend Donthe Lucas, who was clearly involved in this crime. After all, Donthe did invite Kelsie to his hometown on that fateful night and he was the last person who saw her alive. When they realized that the police are stalling with the investigation, the family made a promise that Kelsie's case will not be forgotten until they discover what really happened. They kept the public informed through their Facebook page and eventually managed to reach the Colorado Bureau of Investigation.

Early life

Kelsie Jean Schelling was born on 18th February 1991 in Holyoke, Colorado. She grew up in a tightknit family and later became even closer to her mother after the divorce of her parents. Kelsie was only eleven years old when they split up but she would often talk to her father as well. However, they didn't see each other that often because he moved to a different part of town. After graduating from high school, Kelsie attended Northeastern Junior College located in Sterling, Colorado. She was fascinated with psychology and planned to major in it once she gets accepted to the university.

Kelsie was friendly and outspoken, so it comes as no surprise that she had many friends and was a life of every party. During her time at Northeastern Junior College, Kelsie met Donthe Lucas. He was a star player on the basketball team and the two of them fell in love instantly. Donthe Lucas had a very difficult childhood and he grew up in Pueblo, Colorado which is an infamous place known for higher crime rates than anywhere else in the state. He loved basketball and it was clear that he would be an outstanding athlete even in high school. Basketball players do have enormous salaries so Donthe Lucas did see it as an opportunity to help his family out further down the line.

He was hoping that a scout would attend one of his games and recruit him for one of bigger colleges or universities that had a good basketball team. But his big break never happened. Instead, he ended up in Northeastern Junior College which was alright, but Donthe wasn't quite happy with that outcome. His dissatisfaction was evident even in the relationship with Kelsie. Their romance had constant ups and downs, and the two of them would break up, and get back together which drove Kelsie mad. They did finally call it quits after several semesters, and didn't see each other for quite some time.

After finishing the two years at the junior college, Kelsie pursued her education even further, and she moved to California to attend Vanguard University in Costa Mesa. She was finally able to study psychology full time. Donthe continued to play basketball for Emporia State University in Kansas. Kelsie's family was happy she managed to end her relationship with the troubled basketball player, and they hoped that she would make a new life far away from Colorado. Kelsie was independent and she enjoyed living and studying in California. When she wasn't attending classes, Kelsie worked at a tanning salon with her best friend. However, she did drop out of the college because the school work was a bit too much for her at the time and her only option was to go back home. She moved to Denver in 2012 and started working in a store. Meanwhile, Donthe Lucas was back in his hometown Pueblo.

The two of them started talking once again during the autumn of 2012. It was obvious that they still had feelings for each other, so no one was surprised when Donthe and Kelsie decided to spend the Christmas holidays together. The couple seemed happy to everyone around them, but Kelsie did tell her friends that their relationship was still very toxic. Donthe was still treating her badly, calling her names, and starting unnecessary fights. Soon enough everything will change. A few weeks after the holidays, Kelsie found out that she was pregnant. Shocked at first, Kelsie was lost and decided not to tell anyone for a couple of weeks. But keeping a secret was hard. So she called her mother and told her the news. Kelsie's mother Laura would later say that even though her daughter felt a bit stressed, she was still excited about the pregnancy. Yes, she was young but Kelsie was determined to make it work.

Donthe Lucas didn't take the news so well. Having in mind how dissatisfied he felt about his failed basketball career, it is not wrong to assume that the news about a baby simply solidified the fact that his dreams will never come true. Kelsie noticed the change in his mood and openly told him that he doesn't have to be a part of their baby's life. But it is also worth mentioning that Kelsie confided in her best friend that Donthe was ecstatic to become a father at one point. However, his mind was constantly changing. Kelsie went to see her doctor on 4th of February 2013 and he confirmed that she was eight weeks pregnant. The baby was healthy and doing well. The doctor provided her with an ultrasound of the unborn baby, and she was full of joy. Kelsie immediately sent out the pictures to her mother, her friends, and Donthe. Unfortunately, the excitement will not last forever.

The night of the disappearance

Donthe and Kelsey exchanged several emails on February 3rd, 2013. He invited her to visit him in Pueblo. She turned him down saying that she needs to go for a checkup the next day to make sure everything is alright with the baby. After seeing her doctor on the morning of February 4th, 2013, Kelsie went straight to the store. She worked the second shift and was expected to come home sometime after 10:00 PM that night. However, she was in contact with Donthe for the entire day, texting back and forth about the pregnancy. Donthe told her that she should drive out to Pueblo after work because he had a surprise for her. Not knowing what it is, Kelsie asked for more information because Pueblo is two hours away from Denver, and she would probably be tired after work. He insisted that she would be happy with his surprise and that he cannot tell her anything over the phone.

It is safe to assume that Kelsie thought that Donthe was ready to change and start a family with her. Their relationship wasn't a standard one but it seemed like Kelsie was willing to move past all the negative things and focus on the future. So after her shift ended, Kelsie got in her Chevy Cruze LTZ and drove to Pueblo in the middle of the night. Donthe was supposed to meet her in a parking lot in front of a local Walmart. The surveillance cameras did confirm that Kelsie got there on time, but Donthe was nowhere to be seen. She waited in a parked car for almost an hour before sending another text message to Donthe, saying that she has been in the parking lot for too long and that she would come pick him up at whatever location he is at the moment. She got a reply sometime around 12:15 AM.

Donthe told her that he will be waiting for her in the street next to his grandmother's home. Kelsie is seen exiting the parking lot a couple of minutes after she got the message. She clearly did arrive at the second rendezvous spot, but once again Donthe wasn't there. Kelsie sent him another message asking where is he and Donthe replied that he will be there in a minute. This is the last known communication between these two until sometime before 04:00 AM. After going through the phone records, police did discover that Donthe called Kelsie at 03:54 AM but she didn't pick up. The significance of this mysterious phone call will be revealed later. After reviewing the cell tower pings for both phones, the investigators did discover that they were in close proximity to each other.

The search for Kelsie

Kelsie's mother Laura got really worried the next day because she wasn't able to reach her daughter over the phone. She tried calling numerous times but it went straight to the voicemail. The last message she got from her daughter was the ultrasound image of her unborn child, and Laura wasn't sure if something happened to Kelsie after work, or she was ignoring her calls. Laura contacted Kelsie's friends who told her that she went to Pueblo to meet with Donthe. With no word from her daughter, she called Donthe who picked up his phone and told Laura that he had seen Kelsie last night, but that she drove back home in the morning.

Laura was starting to panic, but she did tell Donthe that she would involve the police if she doesn't hear from her daughter soon. Laura and Kelsie were very close and they did tell each other everything, but she suspected that her daughter kept this information from her because she didn't want Laura to know that she was meeting with Donthe. After all, Laura was aware of the nature of their relationship, and his reluctance to accept the baby. Plus, Laura would probably advise Kelsie not to go to Pueblo in the middle of the night.

Laura contacted the local law enforcement and told them that her daughter was missing. Without any solid leads or evidence, they started asking around for Kelsie. Their first step was to take a closer look at Donthe because he claimed that he was the last person to saw Kelsie. She did travel from Denver just to see him. After checking Kelsie's credit card records, they did notice that the card was used hours after Kelsie's last known contact with Donthe. They reviewed the surveillance of the ATM and noticed that Donthe had the card and picked up $400 from Kelsie's account. They weren't sure if Donthe had Kelsie's agreement to use the card, but that was a felony in the state of Colorado, so he was led to the police station for questioning. He had a lot of things to clear up, starting with the timeline of Kelsie's visit to Pueblo.

Donthe's interview

After being picked up by the police, Donthe told his own version of the story. They did see each other that night and talked until early morning hours. Donthe and Kelsie got into a fight and she felt too agitated to drive back home to Denver. She was also very tired from working the second shift. Instead, Kelsie decided to sleep in her car which was parked near his grandmother's house. According to Donthe, his phone rang sometime around 07:00 AM and it was Kelsie. She wasn't feeling well and asked Donthe to drive her to a hospital. He put on his clothes, got to her car, and drove her to the Parkview Hospital.

Kelsie wasn't sure if something happened to the baby during their argument last night and she insisted to see a doctor before she heads out to Denver. Donthe sat inside her car in the parking lot for two hours when she finally emerged from the hospital. Kelsie told him that she had lost the baby. She then asked Donthe to drive her to Walmart to get something to eat and buy some snacks for the road. The two of them started fighting while they were in Walmart and Kelsie refused to drive him home. Donthe simply walked away and got to his grandmother's house on foot. He didn't see Kelsie later in the day and he assumed she went home. He didn't mention stopping at the ATM to pick up the money during his initial interview.

The investigators did notice a couple of possible leads that could collaborate Donthe's story, namely the Parkview Hospital. Each medical facility keeps detailed records of the patients they treat. After speaking to the staff and going through the data, they have confirmed that Kelsie didn't check in during the morning of February 5th. There were also numerous surveillance cameras all over the building and none of them picked up Kelsie entering or leaving the hospital. It was obvious that this part of Donthe's story was not true.

Of course, the police investigators decided to check out Walmart as well because the parking lot and stores do have surveillance cameras, and they might have picked up something that would be of use. While they couldn't find Kelsie or Donthe entering the Walmart, they did notice Kelsie's car on the parking lot. However, the timeline didn't match up with Donthe's story because Kelsie's car appeared at noon, and not in the morning. Plus, Donthe was the only passenger in the car.

Another surveillance camera which was positioned on the back side of Walmart did record Donthe getting into his mother's car – another detail he failed to mention in the initial talk with the investigators.

Without any proof that Donthe's version of the events is true, they called him up for a second interview. The investigators did have a plan this time - they wanted to find out more about the ATM, and how it fits into his timeline. He told the detectives that he took $400 in order to pay his bills and that Kelsie lent him the money since he was at the ATM while Kelsie was at the hospital. When the detectives told Donthe that there is no record of Kelsie ever being in that hospital, his reply was: "I don't even know what to say right now."

They also presented him with Walmart surveillance video that proves Donthe was the only person in the car. He was surprised with the evidence put in front of him, and before the detectives managed to get him to open up, he decided to lawyer up. He was only charged with the identity theft due to the fact that he used Kelsie's credit card, but the case was dropped. The judge had determined that Donthe did use Kelsie's credit card in the past and it was a normal behavior. However, nobody managed to figure out why Donthe had her card in the first place. After all, if Kelsie decided to ran away and start a new life, she would need the money, as well as her vehicle.

Speaking of Kelsie's car, the investigators took a closer look at the surveillance video from Walmart parking lot because they wanted to follow the vehicle. Exactly one day after Donthe left Kelsie's car there, another man approached the car and got inside by using the key. He didn't break in or steal the car. The man was dressed in black, wearing a hoodie, so identifying him was almost impossible. His body type was different than Donthe's, and the mystery man was significantly shorter. Keep in mind that Donthe was a tall basketball player, so his height would be noticeable, even in a low-quality video.

Seeing the direction in which the car went, the police collected the surveillance videos from stores and businesses which were in close proximity. They put the puzzle pieces together and found a route but they couldn't follow it all the way. One day later, the car was dropped at the parking lot of Saint Mary Corwin Hospital. The man locked the car and walked away. The investigators located the vehicle on 14th of February, 2013 and figured out the timeline. But nobody knows where the car was during 6th of February. There weren't any signs of a struggle that would indicate that Kelsie was killed in her car. Almost all of her personal items were missing, including her wallet and a backpack.

While it is unclear if the vehicle was tested for the traces of DNA, an unnamed police officer who worked for Pueblo Police Department will later say that they did find bodily fluids in the trunk of Kelsie's car, as well as two palm prints. However, no one knows what happened with this evidence and was it ever tested. It is simply another thing which the police investigators decided to ignore in this case. Unfortunately, the whole investigation will be under scrutiny soon after.

Theories

Figuring out a solid theory without too many evidence or information can be challenging. Laura, Kelsie's mother, claims that her daughter was probably murdered and that it was premeditated. The first red flag for her was Donthe's initial invitation to meet him before the doctor's appointment. When Kelsie refused, he knew that he had to act fast. Donthe lured Kelsie to Pueblo by saying that he has something to show her, but he never gave an explanation to the law enforcement about what the surprise really was.

It is clear that Kelsie was alive and well up until the point she met Donthe in the street next to his grandmother's house. This is where the trail goes cold. The activity on her phone stops until 04:00 AM. If we analyze the location of the phones, another theory is that Donthe led Kelsie to a remote location and harmed her. It was possible that Kelsie dropped her phone in the middle of a struggle. Donthe couldn't find the phone in the dark, so he had to call her number. He was very likely getting rid of the evidence.

There is a possibility that the two of them did indeed get into a fight, and that an unfortunate accident happened. However, it is more likely that Donthe planned to get rid of Kelsie, and had planned every single step he would take that night. He really insisted to see her as soon as possible. While it is not fair to put the blame on the rest of Lucas family, the fact that his mother picked him up immediately after he left Kelsie's vehicle at the Walmart's parking lot indicates that she knew what was going on. Pueblo Police Department did stop investigating Donthe, and they claimed they didn't have enough physical evidence to prove that a crime really occurred. But they did receive a couple of noteworthy tips which were ignored and never pursued.

The missed opportunities

The entire investigation of the disappearance of Kelsie Schelling was troubling from the very beginning. While the detectives did not have physical evidence of a crime, it was clear that Donthe was the last person who saw Kelsie alive. In every standard investigation, he would have been the prime suspect, and the investigators would do their best to find more proof that he was somehow connected to the crime. The cell tower pings did show that both of their phones were in a remote area next to Pueblo in the early morning hours.

But there are even bigger missed opportunities that could have provided the investigators with the proof they needed. For instance, Donthe was living in his grandmother's house at the time of Kelsie's disappearance. However, the entire family moved out soon after. The landlord started redecorating the house because he wanted to rent it again. He did hear about the missing girl from Denver but had no idea about the details of the case, or the fact that the Lucas family was involved in any way.

He decided to put the new carpets in and when he lifted the old one, the landlord noticed a strange stain on the bottom. He contacted the police enforcement because he was worried that something bad has happened in the house. However, the police ignored his request to check out the stained carpet, and no one had ever arrived at Lucas' previous residence to pick it up. The landlord ended up throwing the carpet away because he simply couldn't keep it forever in the house and wanted to move on with the renovation.

Another missed opportunity involved a couple of fishermen who were out on a lake on a night fishing expedition. It is important to mention that the lake was located near the Saint Mary Corwin Hospital. As you might recall, that was the spot where the police officers discovered Kelsie's vehicle on the 14th of February 2013. They were out on a bank when a hook got stuck to something poking out of the sand. The fishermen went to investigate and were sure that they saw a part of a human ribcage, as well as a skull.

They were terrified by that discovery and left the area right away. Both of them were reluctant to notify the police because they did have some troubles with the law in the past. But that didn't stop them from telling this story to their friends who urged them to contact the local law enforcement. A couple of months passed before they finally talked to the police, but the lake wasn't searched afterward.

The current searches

Family and friends continued to search for Kelsie even after it was clear that the police enforcement forgot about her case. They created a Facebook group that was constantly updated with new information. Pueblo Police Department did go through many changes after Kelsie went missing. The lead investigator was replaced with a new one who was willing to cooperate with the Schelling family. The Schellings did offer a large reward for any new leads that might help them locate their missing daughter. The reward was $100,000 at one point.

This eventually led to false claims and misleading messages such as the one which claimed that Kelsie was still alive, but was placed into a sex traffic ring after a hired hitman decided not to kill her.

Laura Schelling contacted the police and told them about the message. Since the investigators decided to follow every lead possible, they dug deeper and even involved the FBI. Their experts did manage to trace the message back to Russia through the IP address so it was clear that this tip was useless.

The biggest break in the case happened in the spring of 2017 when Colorado Bureau of Investigation finally got the authorization from the local law enforcement to join the search. CBI did determine that the prime suspect should be Donthe Lucas, and they got the warrant to search the area around his previous place of residence. A large number of police officers was seen around that house during April of 2017, and they dug up the parts of the backyard using heavy machinery.

The search has been successful and the officers left the scene carrying bags of evidence. However, they stated that they didn't find any traces of Kelsie's remains. Kelsie's family released the following statement after the search: "The past 2 days have been grueling and emotional, ending with the outcome we did not hope for. Kelsie is still missing. There is no way for me to convey to you all the pain that I feel right now. Sincere, heartfelt thanks goes out to the members of Pueblo PD, CBI and Parks & Rec who worked so hard on this search for Kelsie. This was a physically demanding excavation for them and we witnessed how hard they worked. Despite all the issues we have had in the past, the new leadership over Kelsie's case from PPD and active involvement from CBI is giving us hope that an effective investigation is finally taking place."

The case is still active and the police didn't arrest Donthe. But the positive changes are happening and Kelsie's family is certain that they will find the answers they are looking for now that the investigation is finally moving forward.

THE DISAPPEARANCE OF BRITTANEE DREXEL

85

FAITH TORINO

Brittanee Drexel disappeared from Myrtle Beach, SC while on spring break on April 25, 2009. She was 17 at the time and traveled without receiving parental consent. She told her mother that she was staying at a friend's house near their home in Rochester, New York. Brittanee's mother, Dawn, then learned where she really was when her boyfriend, John, called her after he suspected something had happened to Brittanee. Her parents immediately grew angry, scared, and devastated when they received word that their daughter was missing.

Brittanee was born on October 7th, 1991 and lived in Rochester, New York. She moved frequently during her youth as her father was in the military. She was a junior at Gates-Chili High school and the year was a rough one with her parents separating. She would live with her mother but still see her father frequently.

She was blind in her right eye and had several surgeries to correct her hyperplastic primary vitreous. To keep her eye from wandering, she would get contacts that made both eyes look the same.

Britt was described by friends and family as a smiling, fun-loving girl. Her demeanor had changed by her junior year in high school as she was depressed that her parents were separating. She would sleep in late and begin to skip school. She would overdose two times on her mother's pain medication and both times were fueled by the fact that she had just broken up with her on-again, off-again boyfriend, John Grieco.

"I felt it was all my fault," Brittany's father said. "When I was here none of this went on. She didn't ingest as many pills as they thought but still watching her get her stomach pumped was a warning. I need help."

"I remember the look on her face," Dawn said. "She was all red. She was crying, tears coming down her face. 'Why would you do this? Nothing in life is that bad.'"

Brittanee would be forced to see a counselor after the suicide attempt. Still, things seemed as if they were a mess on the home front.

Her parents were separating and her mother was losing her home. But she would resume her studies at school and excel on the soccer field.

"She was fast," her father said. "Her coach would say he'd never seen a girl that fast."

By the time Spring Break rolled around in, she was ready to go on an adventure with some of the older kids she knew. It was a long-standing tradition for Rochester students to go to Myrtle Beach for vacation. Britt wanted to enjoy the night life and lay out in the beach, so when one of her older friends asked if she wanted to come along she didn't hesitate.

She asked her mother first and the idea was immediately shot dawn. Dawn Drexel did not know any of the friends that would be taking Brittanee.

"She asked me and I said 'no'," Dawn recalled. "Then she went to talk to her father. She would play us both. She would say Mom said 'no' but Dad said 'yes'."

Brittanee was determined to go. She pleaded with her mother once again and was turned down. Angry, the two got into a fight and Britt would call her boyfriend to come pick her up.

Brittanee decided to fool her mother. She told her mother that she wanted to stay at a friend's house nearby for a couple of days. Dawn reluctantly agreed but Brittanee headed off to South Carolina instead.

Dawn believed that someone had offered her something, like a "modeling job or some other kind of ruse" to get her to go down there. She had aspirations of being a model as well as getting into cosmetology. With her striking good looks, she would be a shoo-in for success in the modeling profession.

"Her biological father was Turkish," Dawn said. "She had a very European look."

Defying her mother, Brittanee would visit her boyfriend at his workplace and tried to entice him to come along. The young man declined, stating that he had to work.

Brittanee then left with her older friends Jennifer Oberer, Phillip Oberer and Allana Lippa to Myrtle Beach. Jennifer was twenty-one years old. Her brother Phillip would be charged with rape in an unrelated case (charges would be dropped) in 2010. It is believed that these were considered the 'cool kids' and that Britt wanted to hang out and be liked by them.

Britt texted her boyfriend numerous times throughout the trip, telling him about the ambience. She expressed her love for the hot weather, palm trees and the happy vibe of young people finally away from parental supervision. But according to friends and family, Brittanee didn't know the older kids that well.

She also called her mother and lied, telling her that she waswatching movies at a friend's house.

CHANGE OF HEART

Britt hit the clubs with her friends and her mood quickly changed. Her friends began using a lot of drugs and she didn't want any part of that scene. She went off by herself, checking out the local shops and walking down the beach.

She then met up with a friend from Rochester, a man named Peter Brozowitz. He was also in town and staying at the Blue Water Resort with his own group of friends; Matthew Abrams, Philip Watson, Keith Cummings, and Anthony Schimizzi. The 20-year old Brozowitz was a "club promoter" who got Brittanee into Club Kryptonite. The next morning, she would meet Peter again at the beach.

The next day, Brittanee called her younger sister and told her that she's at the beach. Her sister believed she's at the local beach which is only twenty-minutes away. Britt then has a friend to impersonate the parent of the friend get on the phone to talk to her mother. The friend assured Dawn that everything was okay.

Britt then got back on the phone with her mother.

"I'll see you tomorrow," Britt said. "I love you and I'll see you tomorrow."

It would be the last time Dawn would ever speak to her daughter.

THE MYSTERY OF WHAT HAPPENED THAT NIGHT

Brittanee decided she would meet up with her friend Peter that night. She borrowed a pair of shorts from a friend and headed out. She texted her boyfriend John, telling him that she's having a miserable time and that she doesn't like the people she went down with. Apparently, they were 'mean-girling' her after she didn't do drugs with them.

She then received a text from her friend who stated that she wants her shorts back. Irritated, Brittanee walked back to the hotel to return the item.

At least that is what her friends say happened as Britt would disappear into the night.

John then became worried when Britt did not text him back. He texted her a few more times, waited, received no answer then he threatened to tell her mother that she's in South Carolina if she doesn't respond back.

Convinced that something is wrong, John calls Dawn at home. He explained that Brittanee is in Myrtle Beach.

Dawn went livid but her anger soon turned to concern when Britt didn't respond to her own texts or calls.

Everyone in Brittanee's family was notified. Something was wrong. Terribly wrong.

The next morning Dawn, her parents and John all made the trek to Myrtle Beach to try and look for Brittanee.

THE SEARCH BEGINS

Police in Myrtle Beach were notified and questioned the friends that Britt had been staying with. Their answers were all the same, they had not seen Brittanee since last night. Police also turned to Dawn, questioning her about Brittanee's state of mind.

Would she run away? Had she done this before?

There was no indication that Brittanee had motivation to do such a thing. Nor did they have any reason to believe she was doing a lot of drinking or drugs.

With no other leads, detectives turned their eyes on the last person to have seen Brittanee, Peter Brozovitz.

Peter would make an appearance on the Dr.Phil show and proclaim his innocence. He stated that they were in his hotel room watching the Yankees-Red Sox game when Brittanee was engaged in a texting argument with Jen Oberer who wanted her shorts back.

He said she didn't have a problem with walking a mile back to her own hotel.

Brittanee's parents were on the show and berated Peter for not "being a gentleman" and driving her back to the hotel. They also found it suspicious that Peter and the rest of Brittanee's friends did not do more after she was missing.

"I had spoken with Peter that morning," Dawn said. "He was giving me three different scenarios...It's fishy."

Peter responded angrily, stating that he was 'being thrown under the bus.' The innuendos were clear, that even if he had nothing to do with Brittanee's disappearance, she went missing because he didn't look out for her.

What is suspicious is that Peter had abruptly left Myrtle Beach with his friends around 2 a.m, five hours after Brittanee had vanished. They left clothing behind in their hotel room and looked to have been in a rush.

Upon his return to Rochester, Peter hired a defense attorney.

Peter had told investigators that she left his room shortly upon arrival to return the pair of shorts to her friend. The detectives got a hold of the surveillance camera from the hotel and verified Peter's story. At precisely 8:48 that evening she was seen leaving Peter's hotel to return back to her own hotel. She should have shown up on a traffic camera about fifteen minutes away but she never made it that far. She was abducted somewhere along that street.

Police continued to question Peter. The young man stated that one of his friends was told by his mother to return home immediately. This story was corroborated and law enforcement did not pursue the matter any further.

Instead, they now focused on Britt's cell phone.

Britt's last text message to her boyfriend was around 8:58. Ten minutes after she had left the hotel she texted "I'm packing and going to sleep probably."

This would be the last outbound message she sent as then John began texting her repeatedly with no answer back.

But the calls she received from John and her friends were pinged by her cell phone. Every time a friend called, her cell phone communicated with the nearest tower.

In looking at her cell phone records, she was moving southbound. The last ping was received at the Poleyard boat landing.

Fifty miles away from Myrtle Beach and two counties over.

Whoever abducted Brittanee knew exactly where they were going. The place was isolated, a rural country islet that only fishermen or locals would know about.

This was not the kind of place a seventeen-year-old girl would go to on Spring Break.

The investigators launched their search in the area that was about four miles in radius. Unfortunately, the terrain was treacherous. Alligators, wild hogs, snakes and biting insects the size of golf balls populated the area looking for their next meal.

Four-wheelers were brought in to keep the alligators away from the sniffing cadaver dogs. Investigators came to the site armed to shoot any wild hogs that came near.

"If her body is here," one investigator told Dawn in an ominous tone. "She would be eaten within six hours."

The search was frantic in the beginning but investigators seemed to lose hope after a few days passed. Britt's family returned home to Rochester with sunken hearts.

Brittanee's little brother chastized her friend upon their returning, stating "I thought you were bringing Brittanee back!"

Eight months later, police still had no promising leads. They would get an anonymous tip to check out an area a few miles north of the original search area near the Scantee River.

Once again, they came up with nothing. But a couple out fishing found a pair of sunglasses that looked as if they would belong to a teenage girl.

Neither her parents nor her boyfriend recognized the sunglasses as belonging to Brittanee. A DNA test was performed on the glasses and nothing was found.

Her mother continued to believe that she's alive.

"I think she was taken and held against her well," Dawn said. "I think she has become the victim of human trafficking."

Investigators and reporters shot down the notion, however. Typically, human trafficking occurs where the victim has a language barrier and Myrtle Beach was not exactly a hot bed for that type of crime. The police did not rule it out but it is low on their list of possibilities.

From 1997 to 2010, South Carolina has reported 12 cases of documented sex tracking. All were women, according to Doors to Freedom, an organization that helps victims of sex trafficking.

A few months later, police would receive some cell phone footage of Brittanee shot by a young man she had met. There were a group of teens antagonizing her and she wanted the young man's help to hang out with her so they would stop. He shot some footage of her sitting by herself, texting her boyfriend. He has since been cleared of any suspicion as he did have an alibi.

Pressed for suspects, law enforcement looked at every possible lead.

Three years later, authorities identified fifty-one year old Raymond Moody as a person of interest. They obtained a search warrant for a Georgetown motel room where Moody rented out at the time of Brittanee's disappearance. They noted that Moody had received a traffic ticket in Surfside beach just one day after Brittanee went missing.

Moody was a a registered sex offender, having raped a nine-year old girl in 1983. He was released in June of 2004. But Moody did not cooperate with investigators and remained tight-lipped under interrogation.

He is also a suspect in the case of Crystal Soles who disappeared in January of 2005.

"We've heard his name before," Dawn Drexel said. "It's a possibility the cases are connected. We don't know what happened to Crystal or Brittanee."

Moody lived in an area where Brittanee's cell phone last pinged. He was referred to as "Mr.Clean" because of his resemblance to the bald character in the Mr. Clean commercials. He has not been mentioned in any police reports since 2012, however.

The FBI would get involved and offer their belief that Brittanee was abducted and taken to a "stash house" where she was raped and then murdered. Her body was then wrapped in plastic and she was thrown into an alligator pit where her body would presumably be eaten.

This narrative was offered by FBI Agent Gerrick Munoz who obtained the informaton from an inmate named Taquan Brown. Brown is serving a 25-year sentence for a different case but stated he was present during Britt's last moments.

He said he had seen Britt when he visited a "stash house" which was a moniker used by drug dealers to describe a place where they stashed weapons, money or drugs.

Brown stated that Taylor picked Britt up in Myrtle Beach and took her to McClellanville. Once there he "showed her off, introduced her to some other friend that were there…they ended up tricking her out with some of their friends, offering her to them and getting a human trafficking situation."

The stash house was in the McClellanville area, the last location where Britt's cell phone was pinged.

Brown told the officials that he saw Da'Shaun Taylor, who was 16 years old at the time, and several other men "sexually abusing Brittanee Drexel."

Brown then claimed he went to the backyard to give Da'Shaun's father money.

During this time, Britt tried to escape. She was caught by one of the men who "pistol whipped" her across the head. She was then taken back inside the house.

Brown stated that he heard two gunshots and then saw the woman being wrapped up and removed from the home.

The FBI agent revealed that "several witnesses" have told him that she was dumped in a pond that was filled with alligators.

Taylor has since been convicted of robbery in 2011 and could face a life sentence. He stated that he knows nothing of Britt's case and with the lack of evidence he has not faced any charges in her disappearance.

Chad Drexel, however, thinks Taylor may have been involved.

He recalled a time when he was out handing out Brittanee's missing person fliers and handed it to Taylor who was in his car.

"I gave him the flier," Chad said. "He had a car full of brothers, friends. He handed the flier to one guy in the back seat. They all laughed and then drove away and threw the flier out the window."

"I got mad. I said 'There's something about this guy…'"

After the information was released to the public, Taylor's mother, Reverend Joanne Taylor, immediately defended her son.

She stated that he had already served his time for the robbery (a McDonald's restaurant) and that he was a "great kid" that was only

16 years old at the time of Brittanee's disappearance. During her son's hearing, Taylor's mother took the stand and said the following:

"And I want to say that at the time of this alleged abduction, he was 16 years old. I was never a mother thatwould let my kids run loosely, and definitely not with the father, you know, out to do things. I kept great hold on him. I am a pastor of a church. They were in church, they had a strict bedtime, I knew every place that they went. MyrtleBeach would not be a place that he would go at the age of 16. So I just, you know, I ask for your fairness, I ask for, you know, the correct justice in this case. And know that he is not a flight risk. I mean, I teached them good values, I instill in them what few things that have happened, they have exemplified overall what I've taught them. He is not, you know, a flight risk or anything.

Chad Drexel read the testimony and immediately took to his own Facebook page.

I would like to set the record STRAIGHT with a STRONG REPLY to Joan Taylor's comments to the Post Courier in South Carolina this past Friday.

Based on evidence the FBI and the Myrtle Beach Police department has gathered, along with FACTS and SPECIFIC INFORMATION gathered from a team of Private Investigators that I HIRED to work with local law enforcement actively during the case (which will SOON COME TO LIGHT) – we have no doubt Timothy Da'Shaun Taylor played a significant role in the abduction and murder of my daughter.

Of course the mother of Timothy Da'Shaun Taylor is going to defend her son – as a father I can understand a need to defend your children. What I DON'T understand is defending your children when you must KNOW the truth.

Her assumptions and words stated have been verified INCORRECT and couldn't be farther from the TRUTH. We know Timothy Da'Shaun Taylor was witnessed by others (Witnesses NOT IN JAIL) with my daughter – we are just praying that they do the RIGHT thing and stop forward with what they know. Additionally he has been seen and followed to the EXACT area where my daughter's DNA was found. Joan Taylor claimed that the FBI and government are falsely accusing her son because of witnesses IN JAIL?! Well, we have other specific evidence, that I can NOT disclose at this time for the safety of my daughters case, which corroborates these testimonies!! Timothy Da'Shaun Taylor is KNOWN to be involved in dog fighting, bringing drugs to parties, and raping women (mostly Caucasian young women) he either picks up UNWILLINGLY or friends of friends that end up being drugged and taken there. This IS ONLY THE BEGINNING!! There is a TON more "EVIDENCE and HORRIBLE INFO" we would like the PUBLIC in that area be aware of for their safety, but we are unable to disclose at this time.

WITHOUT A DOUBT ....Timothy Da'Shaun Taylor is a suspect in my daughter's Disappearance and Murder! My family and I will be following the FBI's requests to keep specific details in our daughter's case under wrap until THIS HORRIBLE PIECE OF TRASH goes to Prison for Life. After the guilty verdict, we will be happy to dispel these fairy tales that are being spun by Timothy's family. It is disgraceful the way this FAMILY and their FRIENDS are supporting and claiming innocence of a "PROVEN"

FELON without even looking at the evidence presented and the FACTS surrounding the case.

Also adding this PIECE OF TRASH photo so everyone can see WHO HE IS!

On March 25th, 2017, FBI agents called Dawn Drexel to inform her they may have located Brittanee's remains. They are now searching an area 45 miles north of their previous search spot.

After two days, however, they gave up the search.

The case is ongoing.